IN SEARCH OF
The La's
A SECRET LIVERPOOL

MW Macefield

This edition published in 2003 by Helter Skelter Publishing
4 Denmark Street, London WC2H 8LL

All rights reserved
Cover design Chris Wilson; typesetting by Caroline Walker

Printed in Great Britain by The Bath Press

All lyrics quoted in this book are for the purposes of review, study or criticism.

The right of MW Macefield to be identified as author of this work has been asserted in accordance with the Copyright, Design and Patents Act, 1988.

All rights reserved. No part of this publication may be transmitted in any form, or by any means, electronic, photocopying, recording, or otherwise, without the prior permission of the publisher.

This book is sold subject to the condition that it shall not, by way of trade or otherwise, be lent, resold, hired out or otherwise circulated without the publisher's prior consent in any form of binding or cover other than that in which it is published and without a similar condition including this condition being imposed on the subsequent purchase.

A CIP record for this book is available from the British Library

ISBN 1-900924-63-3

IN SEARCH OF
The La's
A SECRET LIVERPOOL

MW Macefield

*For my Wife, son and baby daughter.
No-one else could heal my pain*

Contents

The Two-Minute Manifesto ("Shall I buy this book or not?")... 7

Introduction... 9

Prologue 13

Chapter One: A Secret Liverpool 19
Chapter Two: Way Out 31
Chapter Three: The Uneducated Guru 39
Chapter Four: A New Sound 45
Chapter Five: Boo 53
Chapter Six: The Great Hunt for Ken Kesey 61
Chapter Seven: The Apprentices 71
Chapter Eight: The Enthusiast 91
Chapter Nine: Failure 99
Chapter X 109
Chapter Eleven: Raindance 115
Chapter Twelve: The Oral History of The La's (part I) 127
Chapter Thirteen: The Oral History of The La's (part II) 139

Epilogue 149

Post Script 151

The Top Five La's Legends 155
Acknowledgements 159
Anti-Acknowledgements 163
Bibliography/Further Sources 165
Footnotes 173

The Two-Minute Manifesto ("Shall I buy this book or not?")

So… I'm writing this on the basis you're in the shop and you've got my book in your hands and you're trying to decide if it's interesting enough to stump up for the cover price. If you can bear with me, I'm going to give you the lowdown on the whole thing in less than two minutes so that, even if you choose not to buy it, at least the decision was an informed one.

OK, time's a-wasting…

Do you remember The La's? Their song 'There She Goes'? Want to know more? Great, buy the book, because it's all about someone just like you (me) who sets off to try and track down this obscure but talented band, does it (just about), and even gets to meet Lee Mavers at the end. All the questions you ever had about the band will probably be answered one way or another.

For those of you who don't really know about The La's – don't put the book down yet! We agreed two full minutes, remember? And it's YOU that I want to reach most of all – fans of the band don't need me to win them over, naturally. But I understand that others might need a bit more convincing to part with their hard-earned. This book isn't just about 'The La's' inasmuch as it is about my trying to track them down, almost detective-style, with absolutely no experience of ever doing anything like it before.

Also, I'm guessing and hoping that you are interested in and care about music (at least a bit) – otherwise you probably wouldn't have the book in your hands. Good for you, then: that makes two of us. Three, if you count The La's' leader, Lee Mavers. This is as much a human story as it is a musical one. Few who actually know about the band would dispute that their songwriter/singer Lee Mavers is a massive talent, but also a massively lost talent. A talent in hiding. What happens when an artist seems unable to achieve his goal of meaningful self-expression? How do his goals tally with the commercial realities of the music business? And where is the music (not 'the music' but *the* music) and where are the people who write it not because they want to, but because they *have* to?

These and other issues come stumbling into the light in my book. There are moments of sheer Spinal Tap-esque craziness, but also moments of real poignancy, sadness and frustration, as the story of The La's takes you through the tale of the greatest Should-Have-Been British band of the 1980s, if not ever, a tale where bit-part players include Captain Beefheart, Noel Gallagher, Paul Weller, Dodgy, Cast, Pete Townshend and others.

A tale which in fact still isn't finished, which still could have a fantastic and triumphant ending.

Interested? Well take the book to the checkout then, and let's get started...

Introduction

"It seems there are a few who can say it for the many, And maybe one or two who can say it for the few" – *'Sylvia'*, Ralph McTell

When I read a book, particularly a biography (musical or otherwise), I often find myself wondering: why did the writer choose his or her subject? How did he or she become so *obsessed* (what other word is appropriate?) by their subject that they would spend such a large part of their time – of their *life* – researching and investigating the person or people their sights have settled on? Should 'biography' and more especially 'biographers' be made part of some now-to-be-recognised-but-hitherto-unknown mental condition?

Possibly. What I want to do here is to try to provide a small rationale for the existence of this book. Now that it's in your hands and you are reading it, you might (at least in this case) get an answer to the question I've so often wanted to ask myself.

In the autumn of 1998, my life seemed to be at once both stalled and in a period of change. Stalled because I'd just spent long years studying and training hard for a job which, now that I'd managed to attain some small amount of success, was becoming less fulfilling. I would look at my boss and, increasingly, it seemed that the only difference between us was thirty-odd years, our age difference. We both turned up for work each day with the same world-weary smile on our faces. In the quiet of the office during the day I would, more and more, wish for something different. Not better (or even better-paid): just something which would fill my soul up a little more, something... I could believe in. That's it in a nutshell, something to *really believe in*. You know the part in the film *Jerry Maguire* where Jerry (played by Tom Cruise) sums up his feelings by saying "I hated myself – no, I hated my *place in the world*"? Well, you get the idea.

That's the "stalled" bit. The "change" bit involved me falling in love, *really* falling in love for the first time. Don't worry, this isn't going to turn into a lot of drooly nonsense (there are plenty of books out there dealing with *that*, although I would imagine that the number of those which are combined with musical biographies is pretty small). I will confine myself to saying that it would be a lie if I said that love didn't give me a new perspective, a new way to look at things. "Love gives you wings," they say. Because of that, I needed something to fill up (a bit) the workaday part of me which felt so empty.

I'd bought The La's album some years previously – quite a while after its release, well after the band had slipped from the spotlight. It probably got a few listens, and then went onto the shelf with my other albums, saved for a rainy day.

I love music – I always have – to the point where, in order to be that bit more involved, I play music as well as listen to it. It could almost be classed as an addiction, I suppose. If I have a particular song that I like, I will play it again and again, ringing out all possible emotion until, in a way, I feel closer to the song and maybe to the person who wrote it. It sounds a little bit Zen, but I have friends who are like this too, so I know I'm not completely mad. I'm sure a few of you out there will know what I'm talking about.

Anyway, there sat the album until, several years later, a wonderful thing happened, a truly wonderful thing. Something that happens only rarely, even for a veteran music listener like me. I *re-discovered* The La's album. Have you ever experienced that? You get an album, maybe listen to it a little until you think you've heard it enough, put it away for a while (a month, a year, a decade) and then go back to it? Have you been surprised by how much you *hadn't* heard before?

Well, that's what happened to me: the songs on *The La's* rang out *loud* when I rediscovered it. Melodic, urgent, passionate – particularly 'There She Goes'. The sheer joy – there is no other word for it – which comes out through that song almost knocked me off my feet. There was a connection for me between what I as a person was feeling and the emotion I responded to in that track. In a way, it almost felt as if I had written the song myself – I don't mean that in a literal or arrogant way, just that there was a real sense of the familiar about it for me. The song and I belonged, it seemed.

And then, in a mad moment of... I don't know what, I thought to myself: "Wouldn't it be something if I could *meet* the person who wrote this song, the person who put these feelings down to music?" Not in a starry-eyed, autograph-hunting sort of way, but simply to communicate a sense of understanding from one human being to another, to go up to him or her and simply shake their hand and say thanks.

I can't claim to have had the same sort of portentous dream which Mike Badger had (see Chapter One) but I can say that, from the moment I rediscovered the album, my curiosity about the band grew. I wanted to know more. Of course, as anyone with a mild interest in The La's will tell you, information is very hard to come by. The more I searched, the more I was drawn in to the story of the band – the rumours! the near-mythic tales! (we'll come to most of them later) – until eventually it dawned on me that, to find out about this band, to find the people who once were in it and discover what their story was, *that* would be an adventure. Maybe not something to believe in *per se*, maybe not a long-term design for life, but certainly something worthwhile. I was definitely in the market for adventure.

And so one day I found myself in front of my PC, writing this introduction to the book I want to write, the book I want to share with as many people as want to know. Let me say here, right at the beginning, there's nothing special about me at all. Hopefully, my writing skills will get me to the end of this book. That is the most I'm hoping for. Anything else is a bonus – for me as well as you, gentle reader. I'm just someone out there in the dark, in the audience, staring up at the stage and the bright lights like everyone else. It's just that I decided to see what happens after the house lights go up and we are told that Elvis has left the building. That's really what this book is about. Yes, of course, it is, first and foremost, the story of The La's, of their (very brief) rise and subsequent fall. I wouldn't dream of stealing their glory. But it is also, if you will permit, the record of my attempt to tell that story, to pin down exactly what they mean to me and other fans of the band, to identify their small but perfectly formed legacy. Because I believe that The La's do have a legacy which has been too long lost, tucked at the back of one shelf of musical history. I, for one, would like to see them dusted down and brought out into light, so that more people might make the same sort of re-discovery I did. If only one person reading this book discovers (or re-discovers) the band, then I will consider it all a job well done.

Most biographies tend to adopt a chronological, storytelling-type approach, starting at the beginning of the tale and following through. Why mess with a winning formula? But I do want to change things just a little. This isn't just the story of the band: it's also the story of my attempt to find them, both in a literal and more meaningful sense. What I want to do is let the people who want to tell their story. In between, hopefully, I can fill in some of the gaps, and also tell the story of my search for the band.

Are you ready then?

Prologue

"I've always preferred secret heroes" – Bob Dylan

Right, what we need here is a La's crash course so that fan and non-fan alike will be starting (metaphorically and literally) on the same page. Luckily, the story of The La's can be summarised pretty easily, so this won't take long.

Ready? Let's keep it as simple as possible...

Band. Liverpool band.

One hit song: 'There She Goes' (a couple of other singles went nowhere).

Released only one album: *The La's* (band didn't like it, they said).

Lead singer/songwriter Lee Mavers supposedly 'a bit mad' but also 'a genius'.

Band had lots of different members over the relatively short space of time which was their career.

Disappeared after album release and a bit of associated touring. Acquired reputation as 'difficult.'

Weren't missed too much, at first. Legend grew as more and more realised: 'Hey, they were actually great... actually.'

In truth, when you strip it down, that's pretty much all there is to the story of The La's. On the surface at least, there doesn't seem to be much worth the telling and, to be fair, if I didn't know much about them myself, I would agree. After all, how much can there *really* be to say about a band which released only one album, and ostensibly wrote only one song of any note? It may be that the radio perennial 'There She Goes' is their only gift to the larger world. Although it is indisputably a fine one, is that enough to justify further inquiry?

The answer is yes, but the reasons aren't so easily stated, varied and complicated as they are, as everything about the band often seems to be. The La's or, more properly, Lee Mavers – for the story of the band is his story and the other characters, however important, have at best walk-on parts – is a modern musical enigma. The word 'mystery' is not misused when applied to the jumbled parts which form his 'career'.

Patently talented and, at times, wilfully obscure, Mavers and his music continue to inspire curiosity, inspiration and admiration in successive generations of musicians and fans. Few are immune: The La's can count among their admirers people such as Noel Gallagher and Richard Ashcroft, both of whom have repeatedly credited the band as inspiring their own.

At a time when information about artistes and their careers and, indeed, their personal lives is everywhere, The La's history remains unknown. Reliable information, let alone news, is difficult to obtain. By contrast, stories and rumours are legion.

If The La's didn't exist, you'd have to invent them (at least, the music press would). They were the under-achievers with bags of talent. They started the Britpop snowball rolling back in 1987/'88 but somehow lost their way. By the time they relocated it, bands like The Stone Roses and The Happy Mondays were hogging the limelight, hailed as leaders and innovators, leaving The La's stuck on the outside, looking in, noses pressed to the glass.

Lee Mavers has, intentionally or not, cloaked himself and his music in an impenetrable fog of rumour and semi-myth. His secrecy and reluctance to be heard may yet ensure that he and his band are consigned to that peculiar niche in England's popular music heritage reserved for singular visionaries: Cult Artist.

Widely acknowledged as a songwriter par excellence, Mavers is also known as an enthusiastic critic of modern music recording technology. His unwillingness to release further material commercially – for reasons which are not at all clear – suggests a formidable personality, the like of which popular music has not seen for... well, possibly ever. He is the Great Pretender, the indie champion in perpetual exile, forever dangling the promise of a spectacular comeback... if he could only get it together.

Rumours still surface that Mavers is writing and recording in Liverpool, working on songs reputed to be far better than those already heard; that he hasn't retired from music; that he is, in fact, honing his vision, perfecting the line-up of the band. And yet no definite information seems to be available.

If it sounds like I'm blurring the edges and hedging my bets, I am. There is no easy way into this tale but, to give us the best possible start, let's take a look at the main players:

Lee Mavers
Role: The lead player – our hero. Guitarist, singer and songwriter for The La's.
Distinguishing Features: Ridiculously talented, with a penchant for the 'earthy organic' music. This is coupled with an allegedly 'mystical streak' and a distrust of large-scale commercial enterprise, especially the music industry. Particular gift for spotting flaws in the recordings of The La's.

John Power
Role: The loyal Right-Hand Man. Bass guitarist in The La's.
Distinguishing Features: Unbridled enthusiasm. Curly hair. Nascent songwriting ability which manifests itself in due course. Ultimately destined to part with mentor Mavers and pursue his own path of glory with own band Cast.

Mike Badger
Role: The lost La. Co-founder of the band who left as they were about to achieve greater success. Depending on who you talk to, he's either The La's' Pete Best or their Stuart Sutcliffe (Badger remains very much alive).
Distinguishing Features: Musician and sculptor. Diehard Rockabilly. Knows virtually everyone in Liverpool. Possessed of uncanny recall. A bit 'arty.'

Barry Sutton
Role: Mavers' eccentric heir-apparent (maybe). Sometime La's guitarist – and guitarist with just about every other band in Liverpool over the last decade. Knows almost as

Distinguishing Features: many Merseyside musicians as Mike Badger.

Distinguishing Features: Manic guitar playing. Personality to match. Very engaging. Tendency not to stay in any one band for too long, perhaps following Groucho Marx's dictum. "Internally weird" – own words.

Cammy and Neil (a.k.a. Peter Cammel and Neil Mavers)
Role: Guitarist and Drummer respectively, band members toward the end of The La's' career. Neil is Lee's younger brother. Collectively: progenitors of The La's' most musically solid and satisfying period.
Distinguishing Features: They rock!! Both excellent musicians (Cammy reputedly 'The Best Guitarist in Liverpool') and positive influences. Massive stock of funny La's stories available on demand.

Go! Discs (exclamation mark label's own)
Role: The La's' record label (now defunct). Depending on your point of view, either Villains of the Piece – Shameless Commercial Exploiters – or Tireless Underwriters of Mavers' Musical Eccentricities. Headed by Mr Andy Macdonald.
Distinguishing Features: Specialise in prising albums from the tightly closed fingers of reluctant artistes. Willing to grant numerous 'second chances' to their more wayward signings (i.e. The La's).

The Picket
Role: The La's musical spawning ground (or a big part of it) and a catalyst for Liverpool musicians coming together.
Distinguishing Features: A fair-spirited, generously run music venue. The testing ground for most Liverpool bands of any note of the last two decades.

The La's
Role: The La's' album. The artefact upon which

	posterity will judge the band.
Distinguishing Features:	Much anticipated and much delayed. Its (very) awkward birth involves at least three separate virtually-complete-but-ultimately-abandoned attempts and numerous sessions. Has mysterious cover artwork, which no one, including The La's, knows the origin or meaning of. Probably the most misunderstood character in the tale.
'There She Goes'	
Role:	The La's' calling-card song, their one undeniable 'moment'.
Distinguishing Features	Ubiquitous and undeniably fantastic. Mavers' pension plan. Terminally catchy and melodic. One of the high-water marks of British pop songwriting. Frequently covered by other artists. Ironically, it is, in many ways, one of their lesser songs.

Armed with all this information, we are now ready to begin…

Chapter One
A Secret Liverpool

"I had a good education but it never went to my head, somehow. It should be a journey ending up with you at a different place" – Alan Bennett

Where do you begin? How do you go about finding a defunct band?

I collect a few magazine articles. I'm lucky. One magazine has recently done a retrospective on the band and interviewed a few ex-members. One Mike Badger is described as a founder member: he has apparently given up music in favour of sculpture and art. After some more research, I learn that there's a show of his work currently at an art gallery in the south of England, so I take a chance and ring the gallery. Yes, they tell me, the exhibition is there and, yes, they have a contact number for Mr Badger. They give it to me, no questions asked.

Eventually, I eventually pluck up the courage to ring it, expecting it to be a management company or similar organisation, or maybe an anonymous ansaphone. It's none of those things. Mike Badger, himself, answers. Is it really this easy?

Filled with a sense of momentum after finding one ex-band member so easily, I set off with my newly purchased tape recorder and a bag full of tapes, safe in the knowledge that I've never interviewed anyone before in my life.

Contrary to the popular impression, Lee Mavers did not conceive the idea of forming The La's. Nor did he come up with the band's name. The responsibility for both lies with Mike Badger. He still lives in Liverpool. I meet him one Friday lunchtime in February at his art studio-cum-living space in the suburb of Aigburth. He shows me into his studio, which is an incredible place. Shelves stretching almost to the ceiling are filled with assorted bric-a-brac and dozens of large and small metal sculptures, made out of mainly tin cans and old bits of wood. Several large posters on his wall advertise various Liverpool bands from recent times, all of which Badger has had contact with in one way or another.

We settle down in front of his small gas fire. Much to my relief, the conversation flows easily – to the extent that we have to make a conscious effort to stop talking La's while I set my tape recorder up. I start by asking about his earliest influences.

"Beefheart[1] was the catalyst for it all, there's no doubt about it. In Huyton [*suburb of Liverpool, pronounced 'Hi-ton'*] where I come from... I used to knock about with a band called Neuklon and I got them their first gigs. They were the Huyton punks, and we used to drink in the same place. This would have been around 1981.

"I met Lee Mavers as a result, because he'd joined Neuklon on bass. He was a great bass player...

"And then, time went on, Neuklon eventually broke up and I moved to London, because I didn't think there was anything happening in Liverpool.

"I came home one weekend – in September '84, I think it was – and I bumped into Lee at a place called The Everyman in town. It turned out that, unbeknown to me, he had been living in London at the same time as me, just down the road from where I was!

"Lee knew that I was into Captain Beefheart and... well, I actually *met* Beefheart when I was eighteen, and that, looking back now, is directly related to the whole reason why The La's started. I went to see an exhibition in a Manchester art gallery with a friend, and we got into the foyer, and there was this guy sitting in the corner in a suit and a hat, just sketching in his note book and going: 'Fuckin' shit, fuckin', fuckin' shit...'

"And you could just tell, it was the passion of the man as he was doing this drawing, it was just oozing, you know? I was attracted to him immediately and went over and asked if I could see some of his sketches and he said 'Sure' and he told me he was actually a musician, and I told him that I was too, and he said, 'I know, I'm psychic!'

"We really sparked, and we were with him for probably about half an hour talking and, in the end, his band had to pull him out of the gallery!

"About three months later, I went to a second hand shop and found *Clear Spot* by Beefheart, bought it for about thirty pence, took it home and put it on and it was like 'WOW!' It was like nothing I'd ever heard and I loved it. It was rock, jazz, blues and the balance was exquisite. After that, I had to get everything he'd done. And for me, I knew it was real because I knew the *guy* was real."

And it was Beefheart, albeit indirectly, who provided the springboard for

Mavers' and Badger's musical friendship.

"By this time, I'd already had a dream of 'The La's'. I can't remember the specifics, but I do recall that the words 'The La's' were very prevalent in my mind as I woke up one morning, after kipping at a mate's house in Liverpool. This was around 1983, so I'd had the name since then."

At this point, I asked Badger to clarify, once-and-for-all, exactly what all this "La" (or "la") business is. He stresses that he conceived the original meaning of the name as a vocalisation of the major scale note, i.e. Doh Ray Me Far So *La* Tee Doh. However, as he points out, "la" is also widely used in Liverpool as conversational slang for "lad".

"It's every other word you hear round these parts: 'Alright, la? How's it going, la?' The duality of the meaning, once I realised it, became a big attraction. A less-is-more kind of thing."

While still in London, Badger had made some small experimental forays into music. Back in Liverpool, a friend was compiling an album called *A Secret Liverpool,* featuring work by various local musicians, including Badger's piece 'The Time I Grew Forever'. Shortage of money meant that the covers were made from brown paper and only five hundred copies were pressed. A second pressing of the record featured a different track, 'I Don't Like Hanging Around', which was credited to 'The La's' – the first time that name appears on a musical release. However, this was not The La's as the world knows them, but Badger backed by a band called The Modernaires.

Badger: "They were a group from Chester who had their own little studio and we knew the same people in Liverpool so…" The song has a jazzy, light feel to it, with Badger's gentle voice almost scat singing at some points.

Another five hundred copies were pressed as a result of interest, but then things petered out.

Badger returns to his September '84 meeting with Mavers, and talk of a shared Beefheart enthusiasm:

"And so, when I bumped into Lee and he said, 'Tell you what, I'm getting into Beefheart, la,' I was like: 'Yes!' – because it was someone else who understood. I didn't know *anyone* else who was into him. So we had a little chat, I went back to London and thought, 'I'm gonna go back to Liverpool and form The La's with Lee Mavers…'

"I hadn't mentioned anything to Lee, but it was like I was *so sure*. It was like a wave going forward, the inertia. I didn't even need to mention to Lee about him being interested in joining because I knew that it was going to happen. Sure enough, I came back from London and my folks pick me up at Lime Street Station and there's Lee standing at the bus stop! He didn't see me but we drove past and it was, like, whoa! 'How's *that* for coincidence?'

"Next day, I phoned Lee and told him I'd come back from London and talked about our last conversation about Beefheart and said, 'Are you up for making some music?' And he was like: 'Yeah, Yeah!'

"I was attracted to Lee because he was just *different*, a different person to the normal people you'd meet. He had a lot of character and he also looked dead cool, which when you're twenty-two means a lot. In my mind I wanted to create something that was like 'Rockabilly Beefheart'. Lee had been into Jean Jaques Burnell[2] and had learnt all those mad bass lines... Lee is probably the most talented person with music that I've ever met. He can just do it. It's that simple.

"But he hadn't even been playing guitar that long when we started together! I wasn't playing at all at that point, but I had lots of bits of paper with mad words on, and it was all really discordant and Lee was like: 'Yeah, Beefheart, like...' [*Badger sings the guitar riff*] 'De de de dah de de de dah dah!!' On his guitar, and I started singing some of my words... we really hit it off.

"And then we practised, got a bunch of songs together. Lee wasn't singing then: he was just playing these amazing guitar lines, which really underpinned the whole sound. After a while, we got one of Lee's friends, Jasper, to come down, and another lad, John Timson.[3] All of us from Huyton. We did our first little bit of recording in October of '84 in a rehearsal room in town where we recorded 'Soho Wendy', 'I Did the Painting' and 'Red Deer Stalk'. I then found out about this little recording studio called The Attic – which was actually in a basement! – in the city centre. It was a really basic set-up and young kids who wanted to get involved in music and get an idea of what was involved in recording could go down and just have a go.

"The first proper session we did was in February of '85. We recorded 'My Girl Sits Like A Reindeer', 'Sweet 35', 'I Did the Painting' and an amazing dub-instrumental which Jasper started on the bass, and 'Red Deer Stalk'. We went in about ten in the morning and by the end of the day we had five songs mixed and on tape and it sounded amazing.

"Then, this guy I knew from St Helen's Art College was putting together a St Helen's compilation album, a similar sort of idea to what had been done with *A Secret Liverpool*, but showcasing the work of people or bands at St Helen's. It was called *Elegance Charm and Deadly Danger*. Because I'd been to St Helen's and because it was my mate doing it, we got a slot on the album.

"Each band got three minutes, but we were on the album twice because both of our songs were one and a half minutes long! – 'Sweet 35' and 'My Girl Sits Like a Reindeer' – one track on each side."

'Sweet 35', with a wonderfully gentle, light jazz progression played by Mavers[4] has a strong melodic feel to it, with almost surreal Badger lyrics:

> I'm under the water when I'm without you
> I don't seem to breathe too well when I'm all wet through,
> I'm looking for you through my wet eyes, sinking in your ocean
> Sinking in my sighs...

Badger describes the song's ethos thus: "All the love songs were about being 'sweet 16' or 'just 17' and I thought: 'What happens when you get to 20? Do you just pack it in?' It was an ironical love song, about a love that was more enduring."

The other La's track on *Elegance Charm And Deadly Danger* was 'My Girl Sits Like A Reindeer'. Led by Mavers' insistent fuzzed guitar riff with Badger's off-the-wall lyrics about "his girl", it's a sharp contrast to 'Sweet 35'. The title of the song is shouted by what sounds to be at least half a dozen people at varying points in the song. What's more interesting, though, is that, ignoring the lyrics and singing and slow tempo for a moment, the chord structure is virtually identical to The La's' later track 'Feelin". Badger is swift to point this out and sums it up: "Lee simply dropped all my reindeer lyrics, and there was 'Feelin".."

The album was released and, then, nothing else happened: "We kind of drifted apart a bit afterwards. I think Lee got some work with his dad."

Fortunately for history, the band were in need of a lead guitarist and Mavers received a call from Badger in late '85: "Lee's back in the group and he's playing this unbelievable rock'n'roll guitar, even more brilliant than before."

With Mavers back in the group, things started moving. Suddenly, the stakes were upped: The La's were going to play a gig.

"First of February '86 was the first-ever gig. It was Tony Clark on drums, Bernie Nolan on bass, Mavers on guitar and me on vocals and rhythm guitar, because Lee had taught me a few chords by that time and I'd been writing a few songs."

Badger has a small collection of scribblings in a tatty old notebook, in which, he tells me, he wrote down the dates of as many gigs and important events as he could at the time. Of course, memory has a way of rosying up past events...

"First gig, we fucking knocked them dead!

"We were just completely killer... as we were playing the end of the last song – it was a big crescendo – I was walking backwards while hitting the last chord and I accidentally stepped off the stage, landing on the sound system! It was just like an explosion in the middle of the room, and that was the last note of the first gig! A taste of things to come!"

The following month, the band played an open air gig in Liverpool's Saint Helen's park, now bitten by the live bug and looking to play as often as possible, wherever an offer of a gig might be. However, as Badger recalls, a creative change was occurring in the band.

"Lee started bringing in these songs which he had written like 'Freedom Song' – which I always used to call 'The Reggae Song' because of its rhythm – and 'IOU' which was another really early song, and he maybe also had 'Doledrum' then. So we just started playing his stuff as well, and they were just fantastic. A bit Sixties for me, but more crafted than the stuff which we'd been doing."

I quiz Badger about his earliest memories of Mavers' songwriting.

"He'd just kept it to himself, you know? And then he'd say, 'Here's a song!' And it would just be done. There might be a little bit of work to do, and we might change things a little, just exchanging ideas, but most of his songs were more or less done before he showed them to me. And what would you really want to change on them anyway?"

Mavers' new songs were quickly incorporated into the band's set. La's gigs evolved from Badger singing all the vocals to a sharing arrangement whereby Mavers and Badger would each sing lead vocals on the tracks each had written, while the other supplied backing vocals. Badger was now playing increasingly proficient rhythm guitar.

Once again, Badger's connections proved useful when, in late March 1986, the organisers of the *Elegance Charm And Deadly Danger* compilation put together what was effectively a showcase for the bands who had appeared on the record. Of course, The La's were invited to perform. After that gig, recalls Badger, a review appeared in the *NME*, labelling The La's "Surreal Rock'n'Roll."

The snowball was rolling. Gigs became more frequent. One notable early gig took place in a large mansion-style house near Sefton Park in the city. One of the other local bands playing was Marshmallow Overcoat, fronted by Barry Sutton[5] on guitar and Peter Cammel on bass, both of whom would later join The La's – although at different times. Also in the crowd that evening was Paul Hemmings, another La's guitarist-to-be.

Further gigging – mainly arranged by Badger – ensued. With the increased activity came more new songs from both him and Mavers. The Munro pub on Duke Street in the city became a regular venue. It was popular with the group because it was so tiny that only a small number of people were needed to effectively pack the place out.

Badger confirms the changes in the band's set:

"By then we were playing 'Doledrum', 'Son of a Gun', 'Break Loose', 'Sweet 35', 'Trees and Plants', 'IOU', 'My Girl Sits Like A Reindeer', 'I Can't Sleep', 'Clean Prophet' and some others. Most of these were written in '86.[6]

"From about May '86, Lee and I alternated the vocals when we played live, and it worked great. It was fantastic to sing backing vocals on Lee's songs, because they were so great and really easy to sing."

Then, a little serendipity:

"In June, I went on a scheme which was being run by the council for unemployed musicians. The idea was that you'd get together and play, and also be taught a bit about recording or whatever."

Badger is hazy on the details, but supplies a cutting from *The Liverpool Echo* which reports that local MPs were calling for an enquiry into the local "Fame School", as the paper dubbed it, which was apparently run with motives other than music in mind.

Whatever the circumstances, you can only applaud the Liverpool authorities who, inadvertently or not, brought together such local talent and soon-to-be prominent musicians as Paul Hemmings (later of The La's and The Lightning Seeds), Tommy Scott and other members-to-be of Space, Badger himself and one John Power, aspiring bass player.

It was ironic, then, that the one person *not* on the scheme was Mavers himself.

"I think Lee may have actually gone down to the Job Centre to get on the course," Badger recalls, "But I think that they'd run out of spaces. I was one of the last ones picked to take part."

Although the course didn't exactly fulfil its promise to those participating, it did give the musicians an opportunity to gain some playing experience. It also meant Badger got to know John Power. At the time, The La's were going through a lean patch for permanent members, with the only constants being Mavers and Badger. They badly needed a bass player.

Badger: "John was just pure enthusiasm for anything. That kind of teenage football-supporter pot-head kind of thing, because he was only seventeen or eighteen at the most.

"Pot was also a big part of things. Both Lee and I liked it, and so did John, so it was another common interest!"

Power was subsequently invited for a jam with Mavers and Badger. Mavers, being a bass player himself, was, according to Badger, quite definite about what Power was to play: "Lee sat him down and said, 'Okay, this is what you play.' John went away and did his homework and learnt the bass lines."

Power became Mavers' pupil. The education proved useful, as the future would show. More importantly, Mavers had found someone who was relatively inexperienced musically and so open to influence and guidance.

"It was when John joined that I think Lee really felt: 'Now we're a band.' Before, it hadn't been nailed down: we'd get together and play a few gigs – and Lee and I would write – but it was somehow never that definite. We lacked continuity. When John joined, it just clicked into place."

Along with a permanent bass player, The La's also gained something else they hadn't really had before, a following.

"Whereas we knew a few people in town, me and Lee were twenty-four or whatever and we'd left our gang days behind us, but John was in the midst of all that, so all of a sudden all his mates were, like: 'John's got a band, and he's playing a gig!' Suddenly, there were loads of kids coming to see our gigs.

"Café Berlin was the first gig with Power in July '86," [*Badger's head is back in his little notebook again*] "straight off the scheme. For the next month or two, we were just packing places out, a combination of John's mates and the word getting around. Everything really started to accelerate then."

The La's did not find themselves jockeying for position – or competing for gigs – in the 'Liverpool Scene' because, according to Badger, there was no scene to speak of.

"There really weren't any bands around – a couple, but nothing at that time which you might expect in a city like this."

The new nucleus of Mavers, Badger and Power eventually found their way to a recording studio.

"September '86: we went back into the Attic again and we recorded 'Break Loose', 'Open Your Heart', 'Doledrum', 'Son of a Gun' and 'Callin' All'." This last track was a recent Mavers/Badger collaboration which has since attained a near-legendary status among hardcore La's fans. Badger says he wrote the music: the song has a Spanish feel at odds with the lyrics, penned by Mavers, which have a folky tinge:

> A battered wind, a tattered coast
> The wind did gather like a ghost
> And heavy blows came beating down on me

And then, with almost savage harmonies, the chorus rings out:

> Love is all the world will fall
> This is all we came here for
> I hear the ever-distant Callin' All

If I am love's assistant, then I bawl:
'If all the world should fall, then let it fall...'

Rousing stuff with a strong chorus, almost a call to arms.

Amidst the renewed creativity, Badger continued to secure gigs for the band.

"We managed to get a residency at the Pen and Wig, which was the most unlikely place, the un-coolest place you could ever imagine. It was a street away from Mathew Street[7] and it had a huge basement with nothing going on Tuesday nights, and so we got the gig."

The residency was for mid-November into December of 1986. Gigs were also coming in from other pubs and clubs. The ball was rolling. The band's gig schedule became punishing.

"Up to July, we'd done about seven gigs in total ever. By the end of the year, we'd done over forty. In December alone, we played maybe sixteen or seventeen gigs."

But there was trouble brewing in the band between Mavers and Badger, who by this point were co-leaders. Badger confides that this was almost certainly made worse by the fact that the group was gigging virtually every night by December. The tension between Mavers and Badger was no longer creative. 'Callin' All' had been a high point, but there didn't seem to be the time, nor the inclination, to take it further. Now that they were both just going through the motions, it was only a matter of time... Badger takes up the story as the group is setting up for a gig near the end of December:

"There were a lot of hangers-on. We'd now got a manager, Joey Davidson, who was a friend of Lee's from way back. Lee and I were just drifting amongst it all. Lee's a very intense person, very passionate. While we were setting up, there was an altercation between me and Lee. He said something like 'And as for you, you're going on Monday.' This was a Friday. I thought, 'You what?' So I said, 'Well, you're not going to get that chance, because I'm going [now].' I packed up my stuff and I went."

Subsequently, Badger tells me, Lee came round to see him after the row, and Badger later learned that it was hoped that he would rejoin the band. But his mind had been made up and he walked away from The La's for good that night.

Badger is philosophical about the split now: "I can see how, after all the gigging we'd done that month, we just both snapped. When you're only 24 and in the midst of it, you can't see that. The ending of it, to me, now, seems as inevitable as the starting. I could see that my input was diminishing and Lee was certainly more forthright and assertive than me. I didn't have the will to fight to be in my own band..."

Following Badger's departure, Mavers dropped almost all of his material from the group's set – with one notable exception. 'Callin' All' stayed in The La's' live repertoire following Badger's departure and remained there, on and off, until the slow demise of the band years later. They played it for radio sessions too, with Power taking over what had been Badger's harmony lines. It's obvious that, despite the split from Badger and his differences with him, Mavers loved the song. 'Callin' All' was also one of the tracks on the demo tape which convinced Go! Discs to sign the band only a matter of months after Badger left.

But leaving wasn't the end of Badger's link to The La's. 'Callin' All' was an umbilical cord binding him to Mavers. Such was Mavers' love of the track that, when the group were preparing the album's release, 'Callin' All' was its working title.[8] Badger saw an early advert for the album under that name and made an approach to The La's' record label, asserting that he had co-written the song. Nothing was heard back from Go! Discs but, when the album finally came out, all reference to the song and album title had gone. It seemed that Mavers didn't want to acknowledge Badger's contribution to the band. Wounds hadn't healed enough for the two to reach a compromise.[9]

It is, then, good to hear from Badger that relations between him and Mavers have slowly improved and that, from time to time, they see each other and exchange a friendly word.

With hindsight, the way Badger left, or was eased out of, the band he formed does seem unfair, especially as he had been the one to secure the group many of those important experience-gaining early gigs. Equally, it could be argued that Mavers simply had his own vision of the band, which he was going to stick to no matter what. It is clear that Mavers didn't *need* a collaborator – he was coming up with enough good-quality songs on his own. But it would be wrong to see Badger simply as a latter-day Pete Best. He was the only person ever to really collaborate with Mavers. Following his departure, Mavers would be the sole guide of The La's on their musical journey, a journey which proved long and difficult. You can't help but wonder whether, during the darker moments of that journey, Mavers secretly wished he had Badger back by his side.[10]

The afternoon flies by. Before I know it, over three hours of talking and reminiscing are winding down. I prod for extra information here and there, but it's clear that Badger has told me all there is to tell (or all he wants to tell). He says he feels relieved at having got it all off his chest. He also says that this will be the last time he talks in such depth.

He suggests a few people who may be able to help me take the story further, and then we're saying our goodbyes. He gives me an original copy of *Elegance Charm and Deadly Danger* and I thank him. He points out the small black-and white photograph of himself on the sleeve, hair slicked back. He doesn't really look much older now than he did then, even though it was thirteen years ago.

I hurry out into the early evening twilight, flushed with the success of my afternoon, heading back to the city's Lime Street Station. I slump in my seat on the long train journey home. Today has been an achievement: I've talked to one of the two founders of The La's, and I've got other contacts to follow up.

This is starting to happen.

Chapter Two
Way Out
(Or, a beginner's guide to Sixties dust)

Mike Badger had observed during our interview that he'd never attempted to make any mileage out of the fact that he'd been in The La's: "By the time I might have wanted to get anything out of the fact that I'd been in The La's, I couldn't because so had every other fucker in Liverpool!"

This is a key part of The La's history – a frequently changing line-up, revolving around two constants, Mavers and Power. They never sought to disguise the fact, often joking in interviews that even they couldn't remember how many people had been in the group. Explanations for the high turnover vary. Some left for valid reasons (see John Byrne, later) while others lost favour and were eased out to make room for more sympathetic replacements. Still others left of their own accord, unhappy with the band and/or Mavers (even John Power eventually found himself in this category).

It seems that Paul Hemmings, too, falls into this final group, but we'll come to that. Badger's immediate replacement in The La's, I meet him soon after Badger. Like Mike, he expresses some weariness at having to talk about The La's all over again. He tells me that this is absolutely the last time, and it's only because I'm wanting to do 'the book' that he's willing to rake over the past...

Following Badger's sudden departure, Mavers assumed the mantle of leadership. The band needed a second guitarist/lead guitarist. John Power suggested Hemmings, who was also on the council-run music scheme. Hemmings was a longstanding friend of Badger's but, while this may have caused friction, it didn't stop Hemmings joining his former group.

He recollects: "I was at college, playing in loads of different bands, and eventually went down to the job centre, got onto the music course where I met John. I'd seen The La's loads of times by then, the first time was probably when they played at Sefton Park.[11] I thought they were just fantastic.

"At the time, from what I can recall about The La's then, Lee was really using it as his own vehicle, and Mike got off. And then I heard the demos they'd done, the songs were good and I saw John at some gig. He said, 'Do you want to join?' and I said I would. Then I met Lee and we started having a few jams.

"My mum and dad had this old Victorian house with an enormous barn and that's where we started rehearsing."

With the sudden loss of the Badger-written material, the pressure was on Mavers to come up with more songs. In the event, this didn't prove to be a problem.

"It was quite a creative time, because 'Way Out' was written there, in particular, and 'Timeless Melody', 'Over',[12] 'Knock Me Down' – 'There She Goes', too, or at least it was fine-tuned there."

I can't resist interrogating Hemmings about his earliest memories of this last song.

"I remember Lee came round one morning and played the opening guitar phrase, and I remember thinking to myself, 'This is going to be massive, just massive.'"

Being around at this time, jamming with Mavers and the rest of the band while all this new material was emerging, put Hemmings in a good position to stamp his ideas and playing style on the songs.[13]

While Mavers wasn't looking for another collaborator, he was obviously keen to include others' musical ideas if he liked them. Hemmings comments, modestly, that he was both surprised and flattered when he saw The La's later on and the guitarist then in the band was still playing the odd little guitar licks and fills he had originally contributed while the songs were still fresh.

Talk turns to how hard it is to get concrete information about the band, how rumours surround them, particularly Mavers. Hemmings mentions the rumour that Mavers used to carry around a little pouch filled with dust, which had been collected from old 1960s musical equipment suspected of never having been dusted.[14] Hemmings denies ever seeing this. He also takes the opportunity to scotch another persistent La's rumour:

"'There She Goes' isn't about heroin: that's just bollocks, total bollocks. I don't know where that story came from."

Rumours aside, Hemmings was expected to settle quickly.

"I think I literally learnt the set in a weekend. John Timson – Timmo – had joined on drums and then we played loads and loads of gigs, the Pen and Wig, lots of nightclubs, the Picket too."

Even though signing with Go! Discs was just around the corner, The La's were still, as much because of choice and attitude than anything else, outsiders in the Liverpool music "scene". Hemmings recalls that around this time they played the Picket as support for the unlikely sounding Sex Gods. This trend continued:

"We tried to get on *The Tube*[15] when the show came to Liverpool, and they wouldn't have anything to do with us, nothing at all.

"But the gigs continued and things started to snowball. Pete Defrietas[16] started to knock around with us and he became a big fan, got us a bit of studio time – it all helped."

Record label interest had been aroused.

"The phone calls from London started coming. Some company arranged for us to do some free recording at the Picket studio."

This recording was the best yet in terms of arrangements and actual quality of production. Listening to it today, it's easy to see why the band would shortly be signed. Each track is fresh and memorable and captures the sound of a group proud of their songs, with loads of attitude, not caring whether or not you want to listen. 'Way Out' is far more acoustic guitar-driven than the known versions, but that doesn't lessen its bite. 'Liberty Ship', conversely, appears here as an all-out electric guitar rockalong.

Standing out by far though is 'Callin' All'. It starts with a good ten or fifteen seconds of haunting multi-tracked backward and forward vocals by Mavers, leading into the pulsing Spanish style introduction. Whether this crystallizes Mavers' vision of the song (The La's never formally released it), the magic of this take cannot be denied.

Hemmings continues: "A lot of people started coming up to Liverpool from London after the new demos to watch rehearsals and stuff, and then one night we played a gig at the Everyman in town and I remember that it was packed, totally packed out with record company people. That was the night we met Andy Macdonald."

Macdonald ran Go! Discs and was, according to Hemmings, ecstatic about the band and their performance that night. Mavers was won over by him, and the band signed. Almost immediately, Go! Discs moved the group down to London to rehearse before starting to record.

"We were all living in this house in Hammersmith, I think, but it wasn't that good: everyone was living on top of each other and you couldn't really make any noise because of the neighbours. It just wasn't happening."

The band did manage to do some recording, sessions which yielded what was to become The La's' first single 'Way Out' and two of that single's support tracks, 'Endless' and 'Knock Me Down'.

The sessions were productive, but Hemmings had misgivings:

"In a way, with the recording, it wasn't really happening. The early demos and recording 'Over' had all been done during a very creative time, which I think had peaked when Mike [Badger] had been in the band. It's hard when you're repeatedly trying to capture in the studio something that had a great degree of spontaneity to it, as those early demos did. That was quite frustrating for Lee. You went into studios and it just didn't capture it – you didn't get the same sound. After the London recording sessions finished, we were still playing the same set and I think it was starting to become wearing on everyone."

The band subsequently tried recording in several different places around this time, without satisfactory results. Hemmings recalls: "We went to a studio in Coventry for a while, then that was all scrapped, we went somewhere else and *that* was scrapped too. It just became so disillusioning when everything you did was scrapped. Often, as the sessions were starting, Lee was like: 'This sounds great!' By the end, he was saying: 'This sounds shit, forget it.'"

I ask Hemmings whether it was always Mavers criticising the recordings or whether the band as a whole was dissatisfied.

"A lot of it was Mavers but, then again, a lot of it was shit. It just wasn't there when we'd play it back."

Amidst this, the first La's single came out. 'Way Out' was released in October 1987, with an accompanying video which featured – appropriately, given the song's waltz tempo – a fairground carousel backdrop, all lit up at night with the band in front of a big Ferris wheel. This was intercut with other footage of the band playing the song in what appears to be their rehearsal room, and then in a city-centre subway (prefiguring the video for 'There She Goes'). In a self-reverential final shot, Messrs Mavers, Power, Hemmings and John Timson are seen walking away from the camera, past a street sign which the camera zooms in on. It says one word: 'Doledrum'.

The single failed to dent the charts but did get some airplay. However, this was not the version of 'Way Out' heard on The La's' album. Instead, it's based around an acoustic guitar with a proper drum count-in. Quieter than the later version but no less sincere. There is a clear progression from the earlier demos, particularly the Picket demo, to this, their first release.

The debut single, an urgent waltz, was probably thought the most likely to succeed at a time when Mavers was still polishing songs like 'There She Goes' and 'Timeless Melody'. Although not quite the calibre of those songs, what it lacks in variation and melody, it more than makes up for in feeling and enthusiasm. While the production and harmonies might suggest the

Summer of Love, the lyrics deal in the harsher realities of a poor and impoverished existence:

> Give me some money
> 'Cause I'm right in a hurry
> To get a way out of this
> I'm tellin' you this
> That I don't need to miss
> To get a way out of this....

The commercial failure of the debut single needn't be too harshly judged. 'Way Out' simply didn't fit with the music that was being put out at the time. We must remind ourselves that 'Madchester' hadn't yet happened: the charts were filled with the likes of MARRS, Coldcut and 'Yazz and the Plastic Population', early forays into dance and house music. The La's didn't fit into this picture – and probably didn't want to. 'Way Out' was a wake-up call to the self-indulgent technology-focused Eighties. It was a song sung by real musicians, playing real instruments. It was an early indication of the renaissance of guitar-pop in Britain which would peak with the Manchester 'Baggy' scene of 1989/1990, a period during which The La's were largely in exile attempting to pin down their album. Not that The La's were 'Baggy'. They existed in a little bubble of their own, a bubble which didn't cause much of a stir in 1987.

Not that they were totally ignored. One of their earliest interviews was with the NME. It found them revising their history quite drastically but, at the same time, being revealing in a way they rarely were later on. Mavers in particular gave an insight into his muse:

"A couple of years ago I decided that I wanted to write songs. I realised I had the talent for it, like. I had the idea of playing by myself and seeing if I could meet a band, kind of thing…

"Inspiration comes from listening to songs… it's not about being a musician, it's not about being a face. It's just about passing a feeling."

When asked to name a few heroes:

"Bob Dylan, John Lennon, McCartney, Chuck Berry, la – they're all samey and that, la, but his songs, la!"

But Mavers refused to be drawn into any deep debate about his song lyrics:

"They're just words that fit the melodies."

He did however give some insight into rock'n'roll stage fright:

"We always shit ourselves before we go on."

The B-sides accompanying 'Way Out' were two early 'Demo' versions of

'Freedom Song' and 'Liberty Ship' (both featuring an uncredited Mike Badger[17]) and two new songs, fresh from the Battersea recording sessions: 'Knock Me Down' and 'Endless'.

'Knock Me Down' was pure La's-pop, short and bright, with a shuffly beat and loose, funky sounding guitar over which Mavers sings lyrics which read like a blues monologue:

> Well, I got woke up this morning by a chimney-singing crow
> Who came to tell me that I've got no place to go
> So I closed up my suitcase and went tumblin' down the lane…

And then the (possibly slightly tongue-in-check) chorus:

> I'm Jack in the box by name
> Knock me down again
> Jack in the box by name
> So knock me down again

The slightly loftier 'Endless' is a slower track which features a heavily-trebled guitar sounding not unlike a sitar, playing a repetitive phrase which complements the vocals, but also enhances the sitar effect by using an almost modal guitar scale.[18] Mavers' stakes out the song's territory at the start:

> To swim the endless sea of tragedy
> To end up on the rocks so helplessly

And then the seemingly philosophical chorus:

> Of all the places here I came, ever changing, always the same
> I've lost the rules unto this game, ever changing, always the same

This was the first sign of a pattern which would develop: many of The La's' B-sides seemingly had more 'depth' than the A-sides or album tracks. Whether they had more personal content than the other material is debatable but they were certainly just as strong (how often do you hear the word "unto" in a song?). Few of these songs were ever performed live.

Whichever way it's assessed, 'Way Out' was a promising debut.

But things were getting too much for Hemmings, with the band constantly attempting to record the same songs and then playing them live as well:

"It just got to the point where I was sick of it and getting really fed up with it and really burnt out. I'm sure that Lee felt the same way about me. I just wasn't bothered. I kept thinking, 'How long can you keep doing this for?'

"And also, I eventually saw the record deal. We were given so many thousand pounds and, if you're a young band, the first thing you do is go out and buy loads of equipment… in three months, the money had gone. And then, after a great gig at the Marquee in London, we had loads of equipment stolen because nobody could be bothered to unpack the van and it was all left overnight and loads got nicked."

You can tell that Hemmings is at once both annoyed and regretful. While The La's knew where they were going musically, they didn't know or didn't seem to care about the business side of professional music.

Hemmings saw this as a portent, and eventually had had enough.

"It was around Christmas '87 and nothing was really happening and I spoke to Joey (Davidson, the band's then-manager) and we agreed that there wasn't much happening and I said, 'I've had enough.'

"I'd managed to get some cash somehow, and so I just went off around the world…"

Hemmings summarises his time in the band:

"It was a very creative time. Lee was bringing in – I think because he had to – a lot of new stuff. Timmo the drummer wasn't around all that much, so it was mainly the three of us and we'd just sit around with a little ghetto blaster recording the stuff we were doing. I think Lee was buzzing as well and it was great for a while. There's a sort of retrospective appreciation of the band by the people who've left it, of the time *before* they joined. I remember talking to Barry Sutton long after he'd also left the band and he said, "I always liked The La's best when you were in them," and *I* always say that they were best when Mike (Badger) was in them." He laughs.

He doesn't own a copy of the album ("I think I've got a copy on a tape somewhere but I can't remember the last time I listened to it") and doesn't have much good to say about it: "I can tell that a lot of the vocals which were used are obviously demos or run-through takes, so Lee wouldn't be happy about that for a start."

1987 had seen Mavers take control of The La's following Badger's departure. His creativity had blossomed but, despite signing with Go! Discs and releasing their first single, progress had been jeopardised by the problems which had come to light when the band turned seriously to the job of recording.

With Hemmings, a creative sounding board for Mavers, gone,[19] things were hardly on the up-and-up.

It's clear that he hasn't got much more to share, so I thank Hemmings for his time and head home.

Both Badger and Hemmings tell me that they can't put me in touch with any other former La's – which maybe isn't surprising – but both assure me they know a man who can. His name is Phil Hayes, proprietor of Liverpool's key live music venue, The Picket. He, they tell me, knows everything about every Liverpool band, and will definitely know where other ex-La's are to be found.

Chapter Three
The Uneducated Guru

"Home is the place where, when you have to go there, they have to take you in" – Robert Frost

"The pool is where we have to be. The Liver-pool. The Mississippi. The Mersey-sippi" – Lee Mavers interviewed in the *NME*, April 1995

"Someone gave me one of their tapes and we gave it a listen and I definitely liked it a lot. You could tell, although the quality was a bit rough, that it was a better-than-average band. So we arranged a slot for them one night, and they were brilliant, totally ace. After that, it was a case of whenever they wanted to play here that was fine with us."

The Picket is situated on Hardman Street in Liverpool, between the city's two impressive cathedrals. It looks to be a big place from the outside – lots of glass and green paint. Inside, it's a bit of maze, containing as it does a bar, conference centre and recording studio as well as the live music room. I have to knock on the same door twice to be pointed in the right direction for Phil Hayes' office.

If all the various bands in Liverpool from the last few years and the people in them can be compared to strands in an enormous musical spider's web, then the Picket would surely sit at (or near to) the centre of that web.

It's run by Phil and his cohort Neil, two of the most affable blokes you could ever hope to meet. It's a wet Friday afternoon when they show me into their office. The walls are covered with gig posters for bands past and present, nearly all of whom have played at the Picket: Cast, Dodgy and legendary local bands like Small, Shack and The Stairs – bands who never quite achieved the recognition they deserved. The phone rings almost constantly: mainly bands or their managers wanting to organise gigs or other promotions at the Picket. There are plenty of knocks at the door, too – a band comes in at one point, giving away some copies of their first single. They give me a copy, perhaps mistaking me for someone important because I'm there doing "an interview", so I make a note to mention them in the book when I come to this point by way of thanks – Hayley's Cake they're called.

When there is a (brief) lull, I make a start by asking how the Picket decides on its acts. It's heart-warming to hear from Phil and Neil that there are no set criteria: if they like a demo tape, they'll give a band a slot one night and see what happens (this open-door policy goes some way to explaining the constant phone calls and door-knockings). I'm impressed, firstly because they are both so enthusiastic about music and Liverpool music especially, and secondly because they're walking the walk but not shouting about it. That is left to the musicians in the city.

It was this open policy that led to the Picket receiving a demo tape from The La's back in 1987. Phil shows me the small "La's section" of the wall: there's a copy of the album cover, various press clippings and, most enticingly of all, a photo of the band: Mavers, Power, Hemmings and Timson performing at the Picket. Mavers is at the front in the photo, battered acoustic round his neck, leaning into the microphone. Phil reminisces:

"One of the things about them was that they clearly had their own following right from the start – whenever they played here, it was always packed out. Experience shows you tend to find that when they groups first play here, especially if it's their first big gig, then a lot of friends and family will come out to see them. An initial show of support, you know? But then when it comes to the second and third gigs onwards, unless word gets around, then the place tends to be a little empty and that's when problems start. But it was never like that with The La's. Never.

"They were just such a good band, really tight musically, and Mavers was a great singer and presence on stage. And you knew the songs were great."

Phil, who has seen so many bands even he shudders to think, cites seeing The La's as his most memorable Picket moment. Praise indeed.

Neil asks me if I've heard a bootleg of one of the early Picket gigs. I tell him no, so he disappears, returning with scruffy C90 tape, which, he assures me, will blow me away.

It does.

They tell me it was recorded during one of the early gigs the band did at the Picket, while Hemmings and Timson were in the band. We play the cassette on the tape player I'm recording the interview on. The sound quality is incredible, especially since it's a bootleg from 1987. The band blast through 'Son of a Gun' and 'Way Out' as though it was the first time they'd played them (at this time, they *were* still fresh songs.) It's clear that it's an amateur recording because you can hear the voices of the young Mersey scallies recording it:

"Give us the tape for a bit."

"No."

"Why not?"

"Because I said, didn't I?"

And so the repartee continues. At one point, the person doing the recording realises that the end of the tape is approaching and shouts to the band (who are between songs at that moment) to hurry up. Priceless.

The same lads can be heard singing along to the songs they already know. During a pause in the music, you can hear them straining to read the set-list on the stage:

"What's next?

"I can see it! I can see the set list!"

"Well, what's next?"

"Uh… it's 'There… There She Goes'?"

Suddenly, Mavers can be heard: "This is a new song."

And they launch into 'There She Goes', Mavers' acoustic guitar picking out the intro phrase as clear as a bell. Suddenly, just as the song gets going, the sound goes all funny on the tape. I turn to Neil.

"It's always been like that, the tape seems to be going backwards there for some reason…"

The Picket witnessed many of the different La's line-ups. I ask Phil and Neil which they considered the best, but Phil claims a degree of memory loss.

"It's hard to say, but the earlier gigs definitely had that spark… the line-up changed a lot, and people who left could come back. It was like a squad system. Maybe Lee felt that different gigs required different guitarists!"

Neil gives his view: "I think that the problems later on had an effect on the live performances. I recall one of the last gigs they played here – I think it was Christmas '91; certainly John had left at that point – and, well, it was a bit lacklustre. Not bad, but it's just, with The La's, you expect a higher standard than from other groups.

"While they were progressing, we were progressing too and the venue got better sound equipment, although I'm not sure that Lee was too happy with that."

Phil: "I remember the word about them spread like wildfire, and people were then like devotees of the band. The La's were the Liverpool band that every Liverpool musician wanted to be in, just because they had that reputation, that word of mouth, the admiration which they received.

"Lee was always the focal point of the group, because he was the songwriter, but I always felt that they weren't fully formed anyway, that somehow they were organically grown. Sometimes they did seem to be a bit badly rehearsed. It always seemed that they never reached their full potential. Lee wanted to write everything, play everything and control the music totally, so it created a sense of unease in the band, I think. You could see it when they were performing, and it was always like: 'Is this up to Lee's satisfaction?' You always got the impression that they'd come off stage and he'd say to them: 'You're shite, you're shite and *you're* shite. *I'm* the only good one in the band!'

"It was almost like he could never communicate the sounds he had in his head to the other members of the band, and so anyone else playing an instrument is bound to fall short of what he wanted.

"Lee's view is: you shouldn't put out anything that you aren't absolutely happy with and is your absolute best, which led him into difficulties with the music industry, who are market-focused, product-focused. And this has meant that, since then, he hasn't put anything else out. Maybe he doesn't want to, I don't know."

Talking about the demise of the band and their legacy, Phil hits on a viewpoint perhaps not widely considered.

"As someone involved with and concerned about music in Liverpool or whatever, I sometimes think, if The La's had continued and been really successful, then it would have had a positive effect for the Liverpool music scene, in economic terms and also inspiration. Younger groups would have been encouraged by their success. You can look back and see the effect The Beatles had. I'm not comparing The La's to them, but it illustrates the ripple effect that can happen. So, in those terms, it was such a lost opportunity, but I'm also pleased that the album exists because it's a great album. If every musician's got one great album in them, then there's Lee's.

"With Lee, there was always a lot of psychobabble or cod-philosophy – or maybe great insight, who's to say? I always thought of Lee as sort of an uneducated guru, in the sense that he hasn't gone through the conventional route to knowledge – study or university or whatever – but he has a *wisdom* which has been acquired through other ways, other means."

I ask about the last time Phil saw Mavers.

"He comes to the Picket very occasionally, the last time was a while ago, but he comes down to watch bands – a lot of former La's members are still in local bands so that might be a part of it, I don't know."

If, even after all this time, he suddenly rang up and asked Phil for a gig?

"I'd give him a gig, yeah, but I wouldn't count on it and I'd make sure that I had an extra support band, just in case!" He laughs.

The office has been busy all the while we've been talking, so I say goodbye to Phil and thank him for his time. Neil and I leave the office because I've asked to see the live room where the band played so often and he's volunteered to give the guided tour.

You get the feeling when talking to Neil that, although Phil is the big cheese, Neil has more intimate contact with the bands which come to play (he answered most of the phone calls whilst I interviewed him and Phil). Everything is fairly dark and quiet inside the Picket proper, since this is daytime and nothing ever happens until the evening. Neil fumbles for the right key to get us into the live room, and he relays a few of his memories of The La's playing at the Picket.

"I remember the last time they played here which was the Christmas gig in 1991 I mentioned. The band got here about two in the afternoon to set up. They'd hired this massive PA[20] and we got it all set up and then the band had a few run-throughs and then they went off and left Lee, who'd been carefully trying out his guitar through the PA since we'd got it set up. And Lee was like this [*mimes intense expression whilst playing guitar*] for ages and ages.

"Anyway, he was still there and it got to almost doors open – seven thirty or eight – and Lee suddenly looked up and said: 'Nah, I don't like the PA, we'll use the Picket's system.' I couldn't believe it. By this time, there were hundreds of kids outside and we had to take this enormous PA back out, total nightmare!

"Then, another time, he'd bought these really old microphones, real sort of 1940s radio-announcer type thing, you know? He was adamant that he wanted to use them live and hook them up into our PA. It was just mad because there was no way, *no way*, they were going to work in a modern sound system."

He chuckles to himself.

We get into the Picket's live room. It's quite small – rectangular in shape with the stage at the far end, all walls painted black. Intimate is the word, small enough but also at the same time not so small that you feel like a sardine when there are two hundred people in there. I step up and stand on the stage, to try to get a sense of what the band would have felt like during the early gigs, and the audience reaction the first time they played 'There She Goes', but it's not easy on a wet weekday afternoon.

We go down to the dressing room. Graffiti'd on the wall are the names of many bands who have played the Picket in the past. The La's aren't there, but Neil says this is because he eventually had to get the walls repainted, and so any early scribblings by older bands were lost. It's dark and pokey – not really what you'd expect, but then, as any musician will tell you, most dressing rooms are. There's no glamour here.

Neil continues to rack his brain for little bits of information that might help me.

"There was a rumour, I think it was about a year ago, that Lee had gone down to London to do some recording, for about a month or so. But, nothing seems to have come from that so…"

Neil saves the most interesting of his little stories until last.

Among all the names which bands have scribbled on the dressing room wall is the name "The Crescent." He points it out particularly.

"That was a group of young lads from Huyton, played here a couple of times – Oasis-type stuff. Average band. And then the next thing, Lee turns up to watch them, and then he comes to see them again. The next thing I hear, Lee's playing with them, as a band! They could only be eighteen, nineteen at the very most, and Lee's, what, mid-thirties now? I don't know any more than that, though…"

We leave the live room and Neil turns the key. Outside it's still raining. Neil gives me a big smile and a firm handshake and tells me to keep in touch.

Walking back to Lime Street railway station it occurs to me that what started out as a simple job is now becoming more involved with each successive person I talk to. Phil and Neil were very helpful in suggesting further leads.

What impressed me the most about the Picket was the sheer enthusiasm for music which Phil and Neil have and the way that comes through at the Picket as a whole. It's easy to see why so many good bands have found their feet playing there and why the place itself is held in such esteem by Liverpool musicians.

But the thing which really sticks in my mind is the rumour Neil told me about Lee playing with those young lads from The Crescent. What was going on? One thing's for sure, I've got a contact number for them and I'm going to find out! Suddenly, I feel I'm surrounded by leads and people and stories like little pieces of jigsaw. If I only try to understand them and find out a little more, I'll see how it all fits together.

Chapter Four
A New Sound

"If the Sixties and The Beatles had 'a message', it was this: learn to swim. And when you've learned to swim, swim. People who get hung up on the story of The Beatles and the magic of the Sixties are just missing the point" – John Lennon, 1980

"How it started was that I saw Mavers one day and, being into The La's and everything, I recognised him and asked him if he wanted to come and see us play at The Picket, because we had a gig coming up there. He said he might come along, and he turned up on the night.

"So we just had a bit of a chat and we started knocking around after that, we had a practice, a bit of a jam, then more practising, and it went from there…"

It's three weeks since my visit to the Picket. I'm sat in a smoke-filled lounge in a fairly ordinary-looking suburban house in Huyton. It all feels a bit 'student-y' – exposed floorboards, basket of washing waiting to be ironed and not much in the way of home comforts. Joey, Karl and Sean – collectively The Crescent – are telling me how it was that three scallies such as themselves ended up under the tutelage of, and in a band with, one of the finest songwriters of his generation.

They are all young – 19 or 20 at the very most. They are keen to talk when I contact them. Yes, they tell me, they were playing with Mavers and, yes, it was a proper band and everything.

But surely it didn't all come about as easily as they say?

Sean remembers: "It was around the time of the '98 World Cup finals. We just had a jam and he showed us a few of his songs. And then next thing, we were practising all the time. We practised for about four months nonstop, just playing like, every night for hours."

Mavers had apparently decided he had finally found the band he had been searching for.

"We were going through all the material, he said we were going to go and do some recording and everything" says Sean.

Karl interrupts:

"But it seems that nothing's straightforward with Lee and The La's, though. He's sound and that, but he seems to make life difficult for himself, you know?

"Like, he won't stand for no mistakes, none. I'd say that was his problem, he'd want everything to be too perfect, and that would get in the way. I don't really know what it is he's after to be honest. At least, I can't put it into words for you. The whole thing's hard, the whole story of it all, it's hard to grasp."

During these frequent all-night practice sessions, they were exposed to all the new Mavers material. Sean recalls the songs as "Brilliant, honest to god. It's a shame if none of it comes out now.

"It'd be a waste of good songs, because he's talented, very talented. It's just a waste of talent to do one album, when you think of all the talentless people out there making records. The thing is, if you don't get what he's saying, then there's no point, just no point, in going on with it. You could be the best guitarist in the world, but unless you can think like he wants you to think, forget it."

Joey chips in: "It's thinking real, being real…"

Karl reiterates: "The thing is, it sounds simple, but it's hard to work out, and it's hard to play, and it's hard music, harder than pop. It takes a lot of understanding."

Sean remembers that it wasn't just the music the three of them had to grapple with:

"He takes a lot of understanding, what he has to say. Some days he'd just talk to you and it was like 'Whoah!!' – you couldn't take it all in. But then, he's been thinking about music, and his music, for years. The stuff he's got in his head – you know he's clever, but it's not like when you hear other clever people speak, it's different. He's not university educated, but he's clever in all aspects of everything."

I mention Phil Hayes' "uneducated guru" analogy, and they all agree, in a roundabout way.

"It's the best way to be," opines Karl. "That's what he taught us. Like, you could go into some college to learn about music and they could teach you all the theory, all the scales, and you can come out knowing nothing. No one can plant a chip in your head to say, 'Listen, go your own way.' You can go anywhere and learn much about nothing."

Sean says that he did just that, having gone to college to study music but coming out disappointed at the end.

"Nobody can ever really teach you anything, you have to teach yourself, and that's what he taught us, like."

For all their tender years, Sean, Karl and Joey have a maturity about them, especially about music. They have focus and an understanding about music which is rare at the best of times, but especially in people their age.

Sean turns the tables and asks me a question.

"Has anyone said anything to you about a new sound?"

I look blank and shrug my shoulders.

"It's Lee's sound, but he's given it to us as well."

I ask for further explanation and Karl obliges.

"It's like, even tuning in, he's got that sussed. I mean, why's 'concert' concert?"

To keep everyone in tune, I suggest?

"Yeah," says Karl, "but that's just a standard, so everyone's the same. Where does that standard come from?

"If you sit still now, you can hear a ringing in your ear, or if you put your thumb on a jack plug and tune your 'A' string to that, it all sounds boss.

"Even your feedback's in tune. There were times when we'd be practising and an ambulance would go by, and its siren would be in tune with the song, no word of a lie. It's all dead in-depth when you get into it, it's not flash in the pan stuff."

"You're probably the first person to hear about this," says Sean.

So, amazing as it might seem, Mavers and his new recruits continued their practice regime – most days, well into the night, each night.

"It went good for a few months, and then it seemed to die off dead quick, like I think it's done with a lot of people," says Karl.

"People said to us at the start: 'You'll be with him for so long and then it'll just end.' And it did.

"I think he gets frustrated with himself, to be honest, trying to get it out like he wants. And he wants to get it out his own way – he doesn't want anyone doing anything for him, even the mixing, he wants to do it all himself, produce it on his own label."

Joey chips in again:

"It's hard to describe it in words, those months, you had to be there. I've got a tape of us all rehearsing upstairs and you can hear Lee shout 'This is destiny!' on it while we're playing."

Joey disappears at the urging of Sean and Karl to go and find the tape. While he's gone, I run through some quickfire questions with Sean and Karl, who are clearly the most talkative. First and most obvious question, did they talk about The La's with Mavers?

Karl: "Yeah, we had a chat about it, like. But he didn't want to know about it in a way, he didn't want to know about the past, he'd had enough of it. He said that it all went wrong and he was just trying to get the sound out. That everyone started to get on top of each other. The album didn't come out how he wanted it to sound, he wanted it to sound clear."

Sean gives his solution to the problem:

"If I was with Lee, I'd just get him to do everything on his own."

What's stopping him doing that?

"Himself? I don't know. Well, nothing, but he's got his family now, he's got four kids, a house, they're what he needs..."

Karl jumps in at this point.

"That's his own perfection. But sometimes it was just stupid, because what he would want would take, like, three years of solid practice to get. And he'd want it in a week. Himself was stopping himself."

I ask them about the practices.

Sean: "The second jam I think it was, we started at eight in the evening and finished at six the next morning! Then, the next time, he showed us all the proper guitar bits to 'There She Goes', and here's us thinking: 'It's Lee! Lee's showing us how to play 'There She Goes'!!!' And we played it with him, and he said it was the best he'd ever heard it. 'Feelin', as well. He was made up."

"But he wanted it to be too tight," reflects Karl. "In just four months, you can't do it. Plus, we were only seventeen at the time, and it was a bit hard. I mean, we'd just started our band for a bit of a laugh really..."

"The time we had with Lee was just pure eye-opening. You just realised what was happening. We were going down the wrong direction, the same path as everyone else goes down."

What path?

"Just... [*pauses to think*]... guitar-based bands, they all sound the same, think the same, play the same. But songs like 'Feelin' or 'Way Out' sound great, they're really special and they don't come along every day.

"Take Oasis: it's all guitars, really muffled, you can't even pick a chord out, but Lee said, 'You don't need pedals or effects, just make it clear and simple.' And that's dead right. And you get that the best with four people."

Mavers was apparently sure that they'd all go the distance.

"He said that the four of us from Huyton would be back-to-back and untouchable," says Sean, "and I don't think he said that to every person he worked with. He did want to do it, you could tell, and I think now he'd still want to because it's like, if there's a guitar there, you've got to pick it up.

That's just the way it is...

"As soon as you've done a gig and come off stage... it's the best feeling you'll ever have in your life. Now he's had that, it'll be on him until he dies, and to do everything he's done and then to come back here, and not do it anymore. And he could still do it – we've heard the songs. It must do his head in."

Sean recalls his last conversation with Mavers.

"I asked him what he was going to do with his songs, and he said he was going to keep them there with him, and that makes him happy... and, if that makes him happy, then I'm happy for him, know what I mean? And we're not going to rip them off him, we wouldn't do that to him."

They ask me if I want to speak to Lee. I say that I'm not sure, that I want to talk to a few other people first, to get the bigger picture. Sean offers me some advice, in case I do speak to him.

"Being the way he is, he could turn round and tell you nothing, but then again, he might say, 'I'll tell you everything.' If he's ever got a bad mood on, say Everton lost, then forget the whole day. But if they won, he'd be made up with everyone.

"But then again, if you wait for Everton to win before speaking to Lee, you might be waiting a long time...."

They laugh.

I ask if Mavers is surviving on his royalties, since he hasn't put any more music out.

"Well, we didn't talk much about that sort of stuff," says Karl.

"I remember him saying that he wasn't happy about Robbie Williams covering 'There She Goes'! He really doesn't like the music business very much. I remember him telling me that the royalties for 'There She Goes' kept him alive at one point."

We talk a little more about people they think I should talk to, and it turns out that Joey (now back in the room clutching a cassette) has actually spoken to Mavers about my book project.

"I asked him if we should talk to you, but he didn't seem too bothered about it, he sees it all as old stuff now."

So is he still signed to any label?

Sean: "No, not as far as I know, but that's a good point, that: he might be, you know. But the fact is that he wants to do everything by himself, and then maybe give a finished product to someone, but I don't know."

Is anyone still managing or representing him?

"We never saw anyone, so I don't think so. I don't think he'd have a manager, and do you need one anyway? This was all part of what he was saying. He knows how it should all sound, he shouldn't need anyone else.

Look what happened with the first album..."

Sean recalls: "When we started playing with him, he told us not to listen (to the album) because it wouldn't guide us. He said it would give us the totally wrong idea if we used that as our basis to go on."

Instead, Mavers apparently gave them a tape of a gig at the Picket, which – lo and behold! – is the very tape which Neil and Phil at the Picket played for me. This was the basis for the rehearsals.

So did they play the older songs?

"Yeah, he's still into the older stuff, just perfecting it like. Endings and things, little differences here and there."

And the new songs?

"Fucking boss, totally fucking boss," Sean enthuses. "Everything's written – right down to where you should hit the cymbal in some cases! He's got a song... 'Human Race' [*pauses*]... that'd go straight to Number One.

"The first practice we had, we sat there and he said: 'Where's your guitar?' Then he said: 'Right, I know what I can do, show me what you can do.' And we jammed, and he sat there. And when we finished he picked up the guitar and played 'Human Race' and, honest to god, it was amazing."

"The songs that he's got, they're something else. They're worlds apart, it's just his own sound."

Other ones?

"'Open Your Mind': it's only got about two chords and three words, but you could listen to it for days and not get bored."

"'Minefield' is another. And there's one called 'Raindance'. 'Ladies and Gentlemen', too – he has all the names of the songs written down on a blue piece of paper," says Karl. "We were working through them – there are little stars and stuff to show how far we'd got."

Karl starts to play 'Minefield' on his acoustic guitar. It's a gentle, repeating phrase. "I used to sit in my room at night by myself, just playing that over and over and over," he says dreamily.

They never actually got to play any gigs with Mavers as a band, although it was talked about and tentatively planned. And, yes, they were going to call themselves The La's. Now it's all ended, do they think that Mavers still wants to put something out, let people hear these songs?

"I can't see it," says Sean. "I think he's going to stay where he is with his songs, where he knows they are. That's what he said to me."

Joey's been standing by itching to play his tape for several minutes now, so he takes the pause in conversation as his cue. Sean explains how the recording came to be.

"When we started rehearsing, after the first couple of practices, I couldn't help it... I was a fan too, so I got a little tape recorder and set it up behind one of the amps where you couldn't see it."

Karl: "And then, at one point, I thought he was fiddling with the amp, and then I saw that he was turning the tape over, in the machine, and he saw that I saw that he was doing it. And he just winked at me!"

It's a nice scene.

We carry on talking for a while and listen to Joey's tape of their rehearsals, but it all sounds a bit muddy and it's hard to make out where one song/jam ends and another begins.

Talking about the future, all three of them are optimistic and feel that their time with Mavers will serve them well. You can tell they're still a bit amazed by what has happened to them and a little sad that it all ended so quickly. But they are determined to carry on with music.

"We've got time," says Karl. "We're still young so, if we work hard now, it'll happen in time…"

I hope it does happen for them, and I tell them so as I'm leaving. They don't fit the image of 18/19-year-old musicians – they're focused, ready and willing to work and very aware of the need to develop their own vision, their own sound. A New Sound. How many young bands or musicians can you say that of? Not enough. And it seems that the person who has instilled this in them is Mavers, without a doubt.

I can't deny I'm envious: of the opportunity they've had to hear the new songs, to play with Mavers. It seems to have been a good apprenticeship.

It's clear from their experience that Mavers hasn't given up on his muse and his music. If he hasn't, I'm not about to. Now, more than ever, I'm convinced there is a story to tell.

I ponder on the titles of the songs The Crescent told me about – 'Minefield', 'Open Your Mind' and 'Raindance' – trying to imagine what they might be like, based on the titles and the little excerpts I heard on Joey's tape. These are songs that the world has waited years to hear. That wait may yet be in vain.

Chapter Five
Boo

One day, perhaps, you'll be able to buy books which play music while you turn the pages. When that day comes, this chapter will resound to the famous guitar intro for 'There She Goes'. Probably the best-known few seconds of The La's' music, this classic intro was not played by Mavers but by John Byrne, the band's guitarist when the song was recorded.

I can tell that Byrne has left the heady days of rock'n'roll behind him as soon as we meet – house in a quiet village, nice wife and children, shelves filled with various reference books and music texts, one or two classical guitars lying around. In short, we're talking Unassuming Respectability. Since leaving The La's, he has gone on to become an acclaimed classical performer. The rest of his time is spent teaching the guitar.

It turns out that he and Mavers have known each other since infant school. So what was little Mavers like then?

"Lee always looked older than he was, I think. He was always a bit smarter-dressed – more sophisticated, even – than the rest of the children. We became friends and stuck together. I remember our school life being quite violent – there used to be a lot of golf balls flying around the playground!"

However, Byrne makes it clear that music wasn't Mavers' focus during those early years.

"Lee was always drawing. He'd always be doing pictures of things like cars – really detailed and exact. Later on, I think he just sort of came to music and absorbed that as just another thing he was interested in. Eventually, it became the biggest thing in his life. I'd been playing guitar since I was very young, so I was really the guitarist, not him." He laughs.

Byrne's first band experience, with the Cherry Boys[21] ("Because we actually were cherry men – I was only sixteen and the others were about the same age!"), did catch Mavers' attention. Byrne recalls him enthusing about the band. On drums in the Cherry Boys was another longstanding friend of Byrne's, Chris Sharrock, who would later drum for The La's.

Byrne stayed friends with Mavers all through adolesence and saw his interest in music develop firsthand.

"Lee would always be coming over to mine. We'd sit and play guitar once he'd started to learn. He'd play me his latest song that he'd written and we'd jam away." Byrne says that he and Mavers were always free with their ideas. If he had a suggestion for one of Mavers' songs, he'd make it.

"But they all pretty much popped out of him as they were – there might be a bit of refinement, but the essence was there."

It was their close friendship that led to Byrne joining The La's on guitar and averting a personnel crisis in the band.

"Obviously, I'd seen The La's. I went to a few of their gigs and they were great, and really popular in Liverpool. Then people kept coming and going and I remember it was about June '88 and really the band had just got going – they'd only done the 'Way Out' single at that point – and then, for whatever reason, the guitarist and drummer had gone.[22] It was just Lee and John again and I could see that the whole thing had come to a standstill. Lee and I had kept in touch and... well, I always knew that he wanted me in the band. I always felt that, if I'd ever said yes, he would have kicked out whoever happened to be in at the time in order to get me in. I think he wanted me in because we were friends more than the fact that I was a guitar player.

"I'd got my place at the college of music, but I still had to pass a couple of exams to definitely get in, so I told Lee I'd join. If I didn't get into college, I'd stay in the band but, if I did get in, then I'd have to leave when the first term started – which would have been around August and it was June time when I joined."

So Byrne, or 'Boo' as Mavers called him ("It was my school nickname") was in. But a drummer was still needed, and fortunately Byrne had the answer.

"About this time, my friend Chris Sharrock had left or was just leaving the Icicle Works, so I thought I'd see if he wanted to join the band and I remember ringing his mum and she was saying: 'Oh, John, he's had enough. He says he doesn't want to join another band – he's fed up with being in groups.' So I asked her to go and tell him the band I wanted him to join was The La's, and I think he ran to the phone when he heard that!"

So thanks to Byrne, The La's were up and running again. The band immediately started recording. The plan was to record the next single, but they jumped in with both feet.

"We started recording at Woodcray Studios in Wokingham, and we were putting down everything, not just the tracks that came out on the 'There She Goes' single."

With the new line-up gelling musically, Mavers' penchant for experimentation to get the right sound for his songs became more and more obvious.

Byrne: "I think he drove the engineers mad. He'd have them set the recording gear up in trees, in the courtyard, the hallway... I remember one session where Lee got them to close-mike the inside of this big Steinway piano: Lee wanted to try to sing *into* the piano to try to get the reverberation of the strings."

During this time there were, Byrne remembers, at least six or seven finished versions of 'There She Goes' recorded, each one slightly different.

"He lavished such attention on 'There She Goes'," Byrne recalls.

"Before the final take which was *the one*, we had another version which I thought was stunning, but it was very Hollywood – it had 'International Hit Single' written all over it. I pushed hard for that one to be the released version, but Lee wanted to have one more go."

Byrne recalls sitting at the recording desk with his guitar, playing the lead part to 'There She Goes' again and again, Mavers asking him to experiment with almost every conceivable type of guitar ("He'd say: 'Now try it with a Rickenbacker! Now a Telecaster!' We had almost every type of guitar there and we tried out every one, I think"). In the end, he says, he never knew which take of which guitar track actually ended up being on the released version of the song.

You can't blame Mavers for wanting to get the sound on 'There She Goes' absolutely right. After all, it was clear that it was a song with gargantuan potential. There was even debate about how long the guitar introduction should be. Mavers wanted the longer, four-bar introduction (as appears on the album) but Byrne argued hard for a shorter two-bar intro. In the end, Mavers agreed.

Byrne: "I really held out for that shorter guitar intro, because I said to Lee: 'Airtime is short and you need to get people's attention straightaway.' He eventually came round. I didn't know if was overstepping the line because, after all, it was Lee's song. But he always asked me what I thought of things – often ignoring the producers' and engineers' suggestions in the studio and turning to me and saying: 'What do you think, Boo?'!"

Mavers may have valued Byrne's opinion not only because he was very talented in his own right, but because, it's clear from what he says, he spent a lot of time with Mavers, participating in the music, trying to help him realise the sound in his head.

"Often what would happen in a session, John and Chris wouldn't stick around too long if there wasn't anything else for them to do. Chris is a great drummer and works really fast anyway, so once they were done, they often left the studio to do their own thing. But, being the guitar player, I would have little extra bits to do or re-do, and I just wanted to be there anyway, and so Lee and I would bounce ideas off each other."

Byrne recalls being up all night with Mavers for the recording of the melancholy 'Who Knows'.

"It's mainly Lee on that one, but he and I stayed up together to do it one night, just developing the atmosphere on the track. I remember that, during the sessions while we were there, we had to go to bed some mornings because we hadn't had any sleep. The engineers would be waiting around for hours!

"I was always practicing my playing, and by that time I was very into Bach and I would play all these little pieces. Both Lee and John liked to be played to sleep so when it was late they'd be in bed and I'd sit on the floor playing until they fell asleep."

Another nice picture. The La's even *dreaming* music in their sleep.

Eventually Mavers settled on the version of 'There She Goes' to be heard by the world at large. Anyone hearing this version for the first time (the original single version of the song is hard to come by) would be struck by how different it is to the one gracing the final album. After the much shorter guitar intro, the whole band erupts through the speakers. Mavers' vocal and accompanying harmonies are very much to the fore, and so are Power's backing vocals towards the end of the track ("Calls my name, calls my name"). Comparing the album version of the song and this one, there's simply no contest. The chiming guitar and harmony vocals recall the best moments of groups like the Byrds and The Beach Boys and, of course, that other famous Mersey foursome.

Mavers' insistence on making take after take of the song is entirely justified when the final version is heard. At once brilliant, totally memorable, uplifting and yet very simple, Mavers makes the most out of a tried-and-tested G-D-C chord progression and Byrne plays the familiar two-string phrase with a mantra-like fluidity. And everything comes back to the same line: "And I just can't contain this feeling that remains."

The simplicity of the verse lyrics belies the intelligence behind the song's classic structure and melody. Such was the power of the lyrics that the line "pulsing through my vein" was widely rumoured to be a reference to heroin.[23]

Mavers' bridge lyrics are simple yet full of depth and even a little obscure:

There she goes, there she goes again
She calls my name, pulls my train
No one else could heal my pain

The song is two-and-a-half minutes of Prozac-free happiness. No sooner are the final vocals dying away, than you want to hear it again. That, more than anything, is the magic of the song, and undoubtedly why it has been a repeated hit for The La's and other artists as well.

The jovial mood of 'There She Goes' continues in the B-side track, 'Come In, Come Out'.

Byrne recalled: "That was a one-take track. I always liked that song, it was such a groove. I remember playing gigs with The La's and, during that song, people really had a response to it even though it wasn't one of the big songs. That was one of my favourites, even though I felt that Lee bashed it out and then left it – I always felt that song could have sounded a bit better. I also recall spending a lot of time with Chris [Sharrock] getting that off-beat cowbell just right – it was quite tricky."

Rhythmically-driven and reminiscent of the Latin feel of 'Son Of A Gun', 'Come In, Come Out' is quite sparse melodically but makes up for that in sheer groove, Mavers and Byrne each playing complementary funky guitar riffs.

Byrne also recalls some unorthodox Mavers guitar technique on the song.

"On that track, if you listen really carefully at some points, you can hear Mavers using a match box to strum his guitar – the rustle of the matches gave that extra feel of rhythm and he really loved that."

At total contrast in mood to 'There She Goes' and 'Come In, Come Out', the other two B-sides were very downbeat and melancholy, but no lesser songs for that. 'Who Knows' is minimal to say the least – just Mavers and his guitar with some atmospheric background vocals and occasional electric guitar (Byrne, presumably) as well as, careful listeners will note, the BBC Radio Four news pips.

Byrne: "That was my idea, I really wanted to have that warm sound of the radio and whatever was on it at the time being brought into the mix, but Lee kept saying we'd have copyright problems, so it was always mixed down very low."

Instead of heralding BBC Radio Four News, the four-short-and-one-long beeps take on a deeper significance in the context of the song. The radio station continues almost inaudibly but chattering voices can be discerned at different times, as if drifting in and out of consciousness. The lyrics are minimal, but the change in emphasis according to Mavers' clever little shift from minor to major key midway through lends an air of optimism and hope:

> Who knows what tomorrow knows
> Who knows what the future holds
> Who knows
> Who knows…

Unlike its companion-piece, 'All By Myself', which would be recorded the following year, the song ends without resolution as the repeated vocal ("Who knows…") fades, drenched in reverb. Byrne recalls that Mavers' voice was layered with echo: "We just kept putting more and more on, I think we ended up with almost a 'space echo' effect."

'Man, I'm Only Human' was the final track for the 'There She Goes' single.

Byrne: "I remember that was another one-take track – Lee literally sat down with me five minutes before, I think it was, and showed it to me. It was amazing that he could take such time over 'There She Goes' and almost none over some of the others – which were still *great* songs. "

This track has probably the most graceful introduction of any La's song – a single piano chord ushers in two acoustic guitars, one playing the gently lilting chords and the other, played by Byrne, emitting lovely brittle harmonic notes.[24]

Following the 'unresolved' 'Who Knows', in 'Man, I'm Only Human', Mavers pleads outright:

> Man, I'm only human, humble as I can be
> Man, I'm only you, man, I am only me
> Man, I'm only one man, fishing in the sea
> Man, I'm only missing, throw your line through me

The rhythmic plodding pace of the song suggests a military origin, which is at odds with the Eastern scale from which Mavers derives his melody, doubled now and then by a warmly distorted guitar.

Since there can't be many more qualified, I ask Byrne about Mavers the Guitarist.

"I think Lee is one of the best rhythm players, probably ever. His playing is so instinctive and so complementary to the rest of the music, the only comparison I can think of would be John Lennon's playing on the early Beatles albums – just full of life and very confident and creative. He's not especially adept at the delicate work – his fingers just aren't built for it, but he can apply himself to it if he wants to, and again, that's very much like

Lennon was.

"Tuning's another thing as well. I'd always say to Lee: 'You spend half your life tuning the guitar, and the other half playing out of tune!' [*laughs*] He was so obsessed with tuning the guitar to get it exactly right, but physics is against you so I was always suggesting that he use a tuner, and that would be as close as you would get. But, you have to give him credit, he's never given up. Ever. He keeps experimenting and trying different things until it's got to the stage now that he has his guitar tuned quite low – well below concert pitch. In a way, I really take comfort from the fact that he hasn't stopped trying, I really admire that, you know?"

And did Byrne get any inkling of what was to come with The La's?

"I remember John had such enthusiasm and he really liked Lee, so I'm not surprised that he stayed as long as he did. But I remember John being so keen to get out onto the road and everything when I was in the band, he was always: 'So are you ready to get out on the road, Boo, are you ready to knock 'em dead?' But that never really happened and, I suppose, that was down to Lee. John was very keen to learn, always asking me about middle eights[25] and melodies and stuff. You could see that even then, he wanted to learn all he could."

After the recording sessions, the group attended the necessary photo shoots, but the die was now cast for Byrne.

"I got through those final exams and so had to decide whether to go to college or stay in the band. I agonized over it – it actually made me ill! By that time, I was so into the classical stuff that my interest was moving away from the pop idiom, away from where The La's were coming from. I loved the songs, but playing them wasn't much of a challenge to me as a guitarist and it was obviously Lee's band and... well, I've always thought that I need to do my own thing for myself."

The parting was amicable. Mavers went down to London to see 'There She Goes' be cut as a single and to ponder his next move.

Byrne: "I remember that the single came out not too long after I'd left. When I got to college, because it was very classical music orientated, I didn't tell anyone that I'd been in the band for fear that, I don't know, in some way I'd be looked down on or people would be condescending. No one ever asked about it all the time I was there, so I don't think anyone found out. They never knew..."

Mavers and Byrne have kept in touch and are still good friends, and they still get together for an occasional jam.

"Not long ago we had a trip to Amsterdam – it was totally mad. Lee's such brilliant company and a great laugh. Like any true friendship, I think it'll endure."

Chapter Six
The great hunt for Ken Kesey

"To me, what's interesting is the indefinable. It's like recording. You meter everything that's going down on tape, and the lights are flashing, and you've got all these readings, but what you're looking to get on the record, there ain't a meter for. It's that feeling, that groove, that extra exhilaration, that lift, that air. And there's no meter in the world that can measure that. And that's what I look for, what I try to put in a record"
– Keith Richards

"The only way it is coming out [the album] is if we get what we want in the sound, and when it actually does hit the air... it'll start flying, and people'll get it. It'll go down as one of the best debut albums, if not the best" – Lee Mavers *in interview, November 1988*

I'm at work one day in the summer, sun shining outside, me stuck inside pondering some insignificant item on my desk, and the phone rings. The receptionist tells me someone from Liverpool is on the line wanting to talk to me.

"Alright, la, it's Barry Sutton. Are you the guy doing the book on The La's, is that you, la?"

I'd gotten an address for him from the Picket. They thought the address might be out of date. So I duly dropped a line, expecting nothing. That was three months ago.

"Yeah, got the letter, but I've been a bit busy, la...."

It turns out he's keen to talk.

We arrange to meet. A few weeks later I find myself in Liverpool, standing outside the Cavern Club, of all places, watching the Japanese tourists taking pictures of themselves in front of the life-size statue of John Lennon opposite. I'm watching for Sutton, who says he'll be easy to spot: he's wearing blue-tinted glasses. I've seen photos of The La's when he was in them so I'm pretty confident. Indeed, I spot him before he spots me.

We've no sooner said hello than he's leading me into the Cavern Club and out again, then in and out of several other Mathew Street clubs. We're coming out of the third before an opportunity arises to ask him what's up. It turns out he's heard that Ken Kesey, author of *One Flew Over the Cuckoo's Nest* and founder of the Merry Pranksters, is in Liverpool for the day, having a 'happening' in one of the clubs. He doesn't know which one.

We trek in and out of bars for a good twenty minutes until someone we stop tells us that they think Kesey's happening was the night before. Sutton abandons his search. We go to the Munro on Duke Street where The La's played many of their early gigs.

"I first met Lee the night when my old band, Marshmallow Overcoat, were playing a gig at Sefton Park, the same gig The La's were playing at, which I think was one of their earliest gigs. [26]

"Lee was dead into it and came up to me afterwards saying: 'You've blown my mind, I really want a jam with you.'

"And so we had a jam and, god, it must have lasted for sixteen or seventeen hours if you can believe that!

"Now, I was playing guitar in Marshmallow Overcoat, and playing bass was a mate of mine, Cammy – Peter Cammel. The La's were going through a bit of a guitarist limbo period because Paul [Hemmings] had got off just after Christmas '87, I think it was, and… well, Lee, he's always been a bit fussy about guitarists – not just that they have to be good, but good in a certain way – so it did create some difficulties in the band periodically…

"Anyway, Lee and Cammy had been having a few jams, and he ending up joining The La's after Paul left, which was a bit unfortunate because he was in my band! But, I couldn't hold a gun to his head and we were all still mates, so…"

I ask him about the growth of The La's as a band, and his impressions of seeing them live.

"That first gig at Sefton Park, and then the other times I saw them… I know Mike Badger will have said that it was jointly his and Lee's band and everything, and it was. But, to my mind, those earlier gigs were quite ramshackle, quite rough around the edges, and you wouldn't have thought that they would become the band they did at that time. Once Mike left and Paul Hemmings joined, there was a change, in that they became a lot tighter, especially after they'd been playing a while. By that time they had a big reputation and all my friends were bang into them. They were really special by then.

"Lee would come over to my place and we'd jam. I wasn't in the band at that point. We were just jamming for fun."

Sutton claims to have turned Mavers onto Bo Diddley and says this was the inspiration for the song 'Liberty Ship' (possessed of a shuffly-Diddley feel) which apparently came to life during these long jams.

"Cammy was only with them for a couple of months first time around, and then I think he and Lee had a bit of a fall out – Lee's a lovely bloke, a lovely bloke, but it's different when you're in a band with him. Cammy came back later on and joined for good, of course, but at that point he was out. So Lee asked me if I wanted to join, and I did, really badly, but I was with another band, The Walkingseeds. We'd arranged to go and record, so I couldn't let them down and I had to tell Lee no."[27]

But fate was smiling on Sutton, because the guitarist Mavers brought in instead, Boo, also wasn't destined to be a permanent fixture.[28]

Mavers went back to Sutton. This time Sutton grabbed the chance with both hands. But still the line-up was unstable – now the drummer was leaving.

"Ian Templeton had been drumming with them for a while. He's a great drummer – Latin inflections in his playing, which really seemed to suit the music. And at the time, I remember, at gigs Lee was using a classical guitar with a contact mike stuck on, which gave a good sound."

Templeton didn't last long though.

"I don't think he took kindly to Lee's attitude either!!

"After Ian [Templeton] left, Lee convinced Boo and Chris Sharrock to join."

Sutton confirms that Sharrock was widely acknowledged to be one of the best drummers in Liverpool at that time, certainly someone who (potentially at least) could meet Mavers' high standards. The recording of 'There She Goes' bore this out and the first order of business for the renewed line up was to shoot a video for the upcoming single.

Sutton: "There was this idea to try to capture a sort of 'kids running down the streets' vibe which the band had come up with, and I think it did it quite well."

Shot using one small hand-held eight-millimetre film camera, the video of 'There She Goes' is probably *the* enduring image of the band. It's the picture of the group which the public holds in its collective memory.

It opens with a close-up of Sutton's fingers on his guitar playing the song's intro and cuts to the band chasing up and down the Liverpool back streets, interspersed with snippets of live concert footage. In several sequences, the band are seen busking in alleyways, Sutton, Power,

Sharrock and Mavers playing and singing as they walk past people in the street. Mavers even smiles at one point. It perfectly captures both the mood of the song and the ethos of the band – here we are, this is our music and we're going to bring it to you.

Sutton: "It was all done in a day, just us and two guys, one with the hand-held camera." The ragged nature of the video was, of course, directly at odds with Mavers' perfectionist approach to recording the song.

"I remember at the time of doing the video that Lee wasn't happy with the mix and the sound [of the 'There She Goes' single]... I remember him moaning about the sound even then!"

The single had now been released (with an out-of-date band photo on the cover, featuring the now-departed Boo) but didn't even make the top 40, despite a small tour to promote the song.[29] It was the band's second single and the last music released by Go! Discs with The La's' consent.

With a full line-up again, attention turned to the business of recording the group's debut album. For the first of what would be many attempts with this line up, Mavers decided to go back to the studio which had produced the demo tapes he had liked most, the place where he and Mike Badger had first recorded as The La's.

Sutton: "We started recording in the Attic studio, which was pretty basic, but Lee was convinced the sound would be great, so off we went. It was really self-produced as we went along."

Things weren't to Mavers' liking, however. Sessions there came to an abrupt halt. Sporadic gigging continued and the band settled themselves into Liverpool's more technologically advanced (by the meagre standards of the Attic anyway) Pink Museum studio. Sutton maintains that relations with Go! Discs were still amicable at that point, although they were now very keen to see the album appear – after all, the band had been signed to the label for nearly two years at this point, and only two singles had been released. Perhaps it was this concern that led to the Pink Museum sessions being supervised by a producer appointed by the label.

"The Pink sessions were good," claims Sutton, "But the sound could have been better: it was a bit mushy, a bit unclear. Lee wasn't happy. Eventually, I think the producer's brain was mushed! We went over some tracks again and again and again."

It was decided to abandon these sessions too, after virtually the whole album had been 'completed' over a two or three-month period. A couple of tracks recorded at the Pink would surface later on as B-sides to singles, including the magnificent 'All By Myself'. The quality of those recordings can't, in all fairness, be criticised too much. But the band was adamant about the sound they were after.

It seems that, at this point, Go! Discs and Andy Macdonald became concerned. Sutton recalls a visit paid to the band during one of these never-ending sessions.

"Andy came down and talked to us and said that it had been identified – by him, that the reason we weren't happy with the results we were getting was because we were too stoned! He told us that we needed to record and mix without doing any weed and then it would be better. So we were like: [*mimes straight-faced school boy obedience*] "Okay, Andy, we'll only have a beer or two while we record, and only have a spliff when we're finished." I mean, it just wasn't going to happen!

"Then, after he'd gone, I started to skin up a spliff, and shit! Andy came back in! He'd forgotten his suitcase or something and he saw what was going on and he was going off his head: [*Sutton mimes total rage*] 'You're all off the label! That's it! I've had enough!'

We both laugh, but Sutton suddenly becomes very intense.

"But it wasn't like we were just pissing money away on drugs or whatever, not at all. Yeah, we all liked our weed, but no hard stuff. What drove us was the *music*. This guy [Mavers] had a vision and we were striving for that. It was killing us *and him* that, for whatever reason, we weren't getting the result we wanted.

"I know so many people who've signed to a label and say to them, 'Right, I've signed, what do you want me to do?' They really are like that. But not Lee. Also, he had an artistic control clause in the recording contract, so each time he wasn't happy, he would say so. If they didn't like it, well, tough.

"Lee's view is: 'Okay, so you're an artist or a musician or whatever, well, how far are you prepared to go to realise your original idea, your creation? What lengths will you go to? Will you be bought and sold?' Because that's what some people are like, they're not artists – they're company employees."

Sutton readily admits that this approach sowed the seeds for later difficulties.

"Yeah, he was cursed, in my view, by his own approach, by his own high standards. It wasn't like we weren't ever going to get the sound he wanted – he'd got it before in a basic way at the Attic and with a few other demos, so it wasn't like we didn't have an idea of what we were striving for. It's just that modern studios, they aren't especially geared towards guitars and recording guitar bands. You can have a great live sound and then go into a studio, and it can literally come out sounding nothing like you. And this is where so many musicians are happy to compromise or just fool themselves into thinking that that is the sound they've been looking for, and settling for it.

"If you listen to Fifties and most Sixties stuff, it's a warm sound, a gutsy sound, it really moves you, and that's the whole thing, *the feeling*, not so much the quality of production – it doesn't take much to actually record a good song. Look at recordings by people like Bo Diddley: they're really rough technically at times, but they're full of feeling and it really gets to you. With digital coming along in the Seventies, it really became hard from then on for guitar bands to get a good sound in a studio."

After the Pink sessions' fiasco, Go! Discs had become concerned. Relations had started to sour between label and band. Go! Discs had spent a lot of money and had nothing to show. Mavers *et al* had spent time in studio after studio and had nothing tangible for their pains. All credit to Andy MacDonald, then: he came up with an eleventh-hour plan.

"Andy told us that he'd managed to get an original recording desk from Abbey Road, I think it was, and that we'd get together at his parent's house in Devon and start recording." The promise of a recording desk which might have been used by The Beatles got Mavers' attention: the idea got a thumbs-up.

It was a last-ditch attempt but it worked. Under the supervision of producer Mike Hedges, the group apparently shone.

"It was the easiest session of them all," says Sutton, "and the sound was totally brilliant. 'Timeless Melody' was going to be the single and it sounded stunning, completely stunning and Lee was like: [*gives impression of bliss*] and Andy and us were like: [*mimes mutual relief*] – finally, we were there!"

The upcoming single release was to feature a B-side track entitled 'Ride Yer Camel'. Although circumstances contrived to prevent its release, it remains one of the most curious of the La's musical adventures and probably goes some way to illustrating the widening gap between artist and label. Sutton recalls that it was recorded in a flat he was staying in at the time. From the recording, it sounds as though only he and Mavers are actually playing (if Power and Sharrock or another drummer are present, it isn't obvious). The only things audible are an acoustic guitar (Mavers) and a distorted electric guitar played by Sutton. Apparently recorded in the same way as 'Over', the track bears no comparison to the latter in terms of structure. Whereas 'Over' might be rough, it is still a recognisable song with a definite structure: 'Ride Yer Camel' is a meandering semi-improvised blues-beast (around ten minutes in length) that would sound far more at home on a Library of Congress recording[30] than on the B-side of a late-Eighties 'pop' single. Feel is everything with the blues. Maver's grasp of the idiom is obvious here. While the playing owes more to the late-Forties Chicago Blues of Muddy Waters, say, his singing is reminiscent of Twenties

Delta recordings – the high vocal whoops and moaning are pure Robert Johnson meets Son House. The lyrics are sparse and possibly humourous ("Get on your camel and ride, ride to the desert outside..."). It's alarming how easily Mavers taps into the feel.

It's unclear whether Go! Discs had sanctioned the inclusion of this track (Sutton says that early pressings of the single were done) but one can easily imagine some reluctance to approve yet another Mavers home cassette recording. Perhaps Mavers, despite the evident honesty of the track, was testing the boundaries of the artistic and the commercial.

In early June of 1989, a jubilant La's gave an interview to *Melody Maker*. They talked about their problems recording (John: "We must have been through twenty studios") and the old desk they've gotten hold of (Sharrock: "It looks like a spaceship but it sounds brilliant!"). There's optimistic talk of the upcoming 'Timeless' single release ("We know it's 'timeless' – that's why we called it that") and everyone gets so excited that the interviewer finishes the article by declaring that The La's will be 'setting the standard for Nineties bands.'

Confidence: the kiss of death. After the completion of the 'Devon sessions' (nearly all those in the know claim that the sessions were, by and large, completed), Mavers once again announced that he wasn't happy. If he wasn't happy, the album wasn't coming out and that, la, was the end of that.

The reasons for rejecting this set of recordings remain unclear. John Power has claimed that it was the best of all the album sessions The La's did. Producer Mike Hedges has recalled that, while the sessions were good, he got the feeling "that Mavers didn't want it to be finished... things were perfectly good enough, but he started to say things were out of tune when they obviously weren't." He has gone on record to suggest that one possible reason for the rejection of the recordings was Mavers being unhappy about Power and Sharrock and their respective girlfriends going off on holiday without inviting him. But Hedges has maintained that "Lee is still a genius, and I think a lot of it had to do with artistic temperament. I think he'd just set himself these impossibly high standards."

A taste of what was discarded can be heard on the B-side of the La's final single release, 'Feelin''. Listed as an 'alternative' version of 'IOU', the tiny print on the back of the sleeve credits production to one 'M.Hedges.' Further fuel to the 'better B-sides' theory, this version of the song positively sizzles, right from where Mavers counts the band in at the start (as opposed to the 'fade-in' of the song on the later album version.) Absent, alas, are Mavers' astonishing, tumbling acoustic guitar blues rolls which we hear on the album, but as Sutton himself commented: "It drives you mad in a way...

I've so many *good* but *different* versions of all these songs."

Whilst speculation and unanswered questions hang over the Devon Sessions, their rejection by Mavers was the final straw for Go! Discs.[31] The label stopped funding the band and wages were withdrawn. Both Sharrock and Power returned from their holiday to find that the album had been scrapped, again, and that this time the money had stopped as well. Both were furious. Sharrock, who had a family to support, couldn't continue with the band for no money, no matter how much he believed in them. He left. Power was furious also, but didn't.

Things started to turn sour for Sutton, much as they had for Paul Hemmings:

"I'd started to get some stick about my playing after being in the band a couple of months. It just became harder and harder, especially when session after session was scrapped. Lee's very intense about music and things started to get strained between us."

"As a musician, if you're playing a solo or a phrase or whatever, and you're told to play it – the same notes in the same order – ten different times with the emphasis ten different ways, and it's *still* not right... eventually, I just lost my way. I couldn't see where it was coming from."

In November, the *NME* "discovered" The La's again (the second time in as many years) in a lengthy interview with the new line-up which found the music weekly declaring Mavers and co "The New Beatles." In a wide-ranging conversation, Mavers found himself talking about his inspiration:

"It all comes back to God for me, whatever it is – not this fella in the sky – nature, change, whatever... for the first time in ages, I lay in bed and contemplated life, I couldn't help it. It was four o'clock and all that and I was scared, la."

Sharrock also confirmed his willingness to join the band when asked:

"I heard the songs and the hairs on the back of my neck were up and I just went: 'Fucking hell!' You *would* go to hell and back to find a band like this."

Mention is made of the difficulties getting a recorded sound the band was happy with. Mavers: "Modern studios and us just don't mix... they put a noise reduction on it – it takes away hiss but it takes away the vibe too, and all you're left with is bare bones."

Perhaps this explains why Mavers rejected the Devon sessions, but there is still a sense of optimism pervading through the lines, although the title of the feature – 'The La's Chance' – doesn't seem so inappropriate with hindsight.

In mid-1989, a La's show at the London Town and Country Club was taped and part of it was later broadcast on UK television. If reports from other gigs are to be believed, it does not truly represent the band live. Mavers is clearly sullen, Power bops away in a little world of his own. There is no communication with the audience between songs (except for the occasional "Thanks" from Power) and Mavers turns his back on the audience for large parts of some songs. The performance is pedestrian at best, except at the very end when, following 'Looking Glass', Mavers breaks his set-list-cast-in-stone rule and the band launches into a new song. The outrageously titled 'I Am The Key' had been debuted on a radio session earlier in the year [Mavers on air at the time: "We wrote this one in the car on the way down, like..."] and won immediate favour: the band began using it as an encore. It gives a tantalizing glimpse of what other unheard gems might be like. Despite the title, the song isn't so much egotistical rather than celebrating the need for others:

> I am the key, you are the door
> I am the sea, you are the shore
> Do you know what you're looking for?
> Do you know what you are?
> 'Cause I am the key
> Open the door, open the door

Meanwhile, the writing was on the wall for Sutton: "If I hadn't been pushed, there's no way I would have left, no way, because I loved the music so much... [*long pause*] but, after I was out, it was a relief because the pressure was off."

Sutton looks away for a while, thoughtfully. Finally he turns back.

"In a way, since leaving the band, and especially once Lee dropped out of sight, I've really tried to pick up the gauntlet he threw down by trying to get, well, a *good* recording sound for a guitar band. Just knowing Lee is a lesson in integrity and I'm trying to continue in the same way."

Talk turns to the future, if any, for The La's.

"Lee's very smart, he knows the way things come across and appear. He knows he's left an unfinished musical statement, and I can't believe he's happy with that.

"I always used to say to Lee that, by the time this thing really does take off, we'll all be settled down with kids and families..." He laughs, then fixes me with a stare and says with an almost conspiratorial tone: "I still believe that it will happen for him, though. Even now. I really believe it, because he's got talent immense. Talent immense."

We talk for a while longer, but it's clear that he's said all the important things he wanted. We part with a handshake and I wish him well.

He tells me he's off to continue his search for Ken Kesey who, Sutton remains adamant, is somewhere in the city having a 'happening', Before I can blink he's gone, disappeared into the late Saturday afternoon crowds of the city centre.

Talent immense.

Chapter Seven
The Apprentices

"It *was* a special time I think. There were a lot of gigs at those houses by the park. They were all mainly student houses which were being done up and so, each time a house was about to be done up, there'd be a hell of party and bands would come and play and everyone would get together. The houses would be all empty and the drums and amps would be set up in the living room or somewhere – big rooms, and that would be the gig. It was a positive feeling."

I'm talking to Cammy and Neil – that's Peter Cammel and Neil Mavers (Lee's younger brother) to you and I. Having been trying to track them down – Cammy especially – since starting my search, it's only towards the end that I manage to find them. They're still playing together (Cammy the guitarist and Neil the drummer) and are in the process of recording material for a new project.

A lot has been happening lately: John Power's hugely successful post-La's band Cast have parted with their record label after the poor sales of their fourth album, and a clipping sent to me from The Picket reports that the lads from The Crescent have signed up to their first record deal. Several La's retrospectives have recently appeared in the music press and their album has been re-released 'remastered' with a couple of B-sides thrown in. I'm not alone in my feelings about the band after all.

We find the now obligatory Liverpool city-centre pub in which to sit drink and reminisce during a wet Wednesday lunchtime. Both of them are very likeable and, although Neil initially seems reticent, he is soon doing most of the talking.

Unlike previous interviewees, Cammy and Neil say they're rarely asked about their time in The La's. "I've been asked about it maybe twice in my whole life," says Neil.

I start by talking about Barry Sutton's early band Marshmallow Overcoat and Cammy's involvement (he played bass). Talk turns to the famous/infamous Sefton Park gig where The La's and Marshmallow Overcoat shared the same bill, which Cammy reminisces about.

"On that particular night, I think The La's just turned up after one of their regular gigs and they had a bit of a play. That was the vibe – people could come and play and have a bit of a jam. There'd be lots of people there, sometimes four or five bands in one place at one time. People could jam until four in the morning and no one would complain.

"For me, that night was just another Marshmallow gig, but I know for them (i.e. The La's) it was a bit of a turning point, kind of the start of it all. Although it wasn't too long after that the big house parties sort of stopped and died away. That summer was a real 'meeting people' kind of time, musicians seemed to be getting together.

"And The La's, it was still Mike [Badger] and Lee at that time but they were a bit special, you could see. I think that was the night when they themselves really felt that things could kick off, really start happening.

"The other thing that really helped them – a *lot* – was that John [Power] had loads and loads of mates and they always went to see the band. You only needed twenty or thirty mates, each with girlfriends and a few others, and you're soon talking a hundred people. So, wherever they played, the place was always packed out. It created that extra buzz around them, right from when John joined. It definitely got them noticed early on."

Neil was a little too young to participate fully in this activity:

"I was still at school, but I've heard it was a boss time and people were sparking off each other and getting together in bands. Lee and Cammy's older brother were at school together, which is where a lot of connection came from. Cammy and me and James Joyce started hanging around and jamming. It was only a school band but it laid the groundwork for things to come.

"And even after finishing school, we continued to get together and play when we could, but it wasn't until The La's began to take off that we had anywhere to practice. But, once they got their rehearsal rooms, whenever they were away touring or whatever, we'd get to use the room for free so it was great!"

But meanwhile Cammy had already been in The La's once, and left. Neil recalls:

"When Timmo [John Timson] left, it was like Lee was on a quest to find the ultimate drummer, and he kept pestering Ian Templeton to join the band. And Cammy joined then as well."

Cammy: "It was probably about six months of me being in the band that first time, with Ian on the drums. I'd moved on from bass to guitar and left Marshmallow Overcoat to join The La's. But I don't think either Ian, me or Lee were that happy with things and in the end it just folded: a very short-lived line-up. I remember Ian had a flat and we used to just go down there every day and have a bit of a smoke and then go home at the end of the afternoon and that was the rehearsal![32]

"It was all around this sort of time that I began to do some roadying for them, because I was always going to their gigs. No one else really had the patience to help Lee tune up the guitars because he *never* used a tuner so we'd have to sit in a loud club strumming away for ages to get the guitars to some kind of fit state. So, although I wasn't in the band anymore, I was still helping out – that's the kind of situation it was. I got a better feeling playing with Neil and James [Joyce] so we just kept on but I still helped out the others."

It was when The La's' career began to move forward that Cammy and newly recruited Neil began to have full-time, paid involvement with the band as roadies proper.

Neil: "I think it made sense to Lee to have me and Cammy because I was family and he knew Cammy already so he could trust us. Plus, I was drumming so could look after the drum kit and Cammy played guitar and bass so he could see to the guitars and bass."

They tell me about their early experiences with the band as roadies. At this point, the previously unmentioned and hitherto unknown 'C' – as we shall call him to preserve his anonymity – enters the frame. C was a La's crew stalwart who did a lot of the driving for the band during the early part of their career. He was, it's clear, a long-time friend of Mavers and, equally, as Neil puts it, "Horrible. Smooth but basically a criminal, but in a way loveable at the same time."

C was living a twilight existence at the edge of The La's' world. Neil takes up the story of his and Cammy's first meeting with C:

"It was our first proper gig as proper roadies – Chris Sharrock had joined and things were starting to move again with the band. And that night Lee had arranged it all. He told us to be at a certain place at a certain time, and the van would pick us up.

"So, at about the right time, this van came tearing down the street and pulled up with breaks screeching – just like in a film. Bloke inside shouts: 'You Cammy and Neil?' And so we get in and I realise that it's C – I remembered him from when I was little and he'd come round to see Lee. And he's mumbling and cursing under his breath all the time – this was the way he was most of the time – and Cammy's whispering to me: 'Who *is* this bloke?' And I'm remembering how he was all horrible and scary and thinking quietly to myself: 'Oh, no...'

"So we're off to this gig somewhere in Scotland and the three of us are *flying* up the motorway in this van. And C starts to skin up a joint on his lap with just his *elbow* on the wheel – and we must be doing at least a hundred miles an hour. He never used to use the break either, never slowed down for corners or anything."

Cammy chips in: "He was amazing at that you know, skinning up whilst driving. I think we timed him once and the fastest he did it was twenty-six seconds or around that. And that was the record. No one could ever beat it."

Neil: "But we were young – I was only eighteen, I think, and Cammy just twenty or twenty-one, and it was scary. He was just that sort of bloke that you didn't know what he was going to do in any situation.

"And so we got to the gig eventually – don't forget we've got to do all the setting up and unloading and stuff – and it all goes OK. Then we're somewhere afterwards – a pub or club – and C starts just virtually assaulting any girl that he likes the look of!"

Cammy explains:

"He had this thing where he'd lick the palm of his hand and then creep up to some girl and wrap his hand over her mouth – ugh! And we were just like... [*mimes himself and Neil looking at each other in complete disgust*]... who *is* this bloke?"

Neil again:

"So, anyway, eventually we need to sleep and we get to the hotel and there's no one there at the reception because by now it's really late. There's this little bell and we keep ringing it but nobody comes. We're all stood there – us, the band, Joey the manager, and C. Then we see the little key cupboard and someone gets the plan: we'll each take a key for a room. In the morning, we'll explain to the hotel people what happened and they can sort it all out.

"I reach over to get some keys – reaching over the reception desk – and there's some guy on the floor, lying on the floor on the other side of the desk! It looked like he was dead, but then we saw the empty whiskey bottle. But we couldn't wake him, no matter what, so it was 'plan A', back to the keys.

"So, somehow it ends up that I've got to share a room with C and our Lee. And we're all moving through the hotel looking for the rooms which match our keys, and because we just grabbed any, people are peeling off – the rooms are all in different parts of the hotel. It gets to the last group of us and we finally find our rooms. I open the door to ours, and it's not a bedroom. It's some sort of office. I start to say, 'We'll have to go and get another fucking key now – all the way back to reception!' and as I do so I'm closing the door.

"Just as the door is closing, out of the corner of my eye I see C diving through the closing gap and I start to say, 'What are you doing?' At that point, I see what C has just seen. At the far end of this office-room, there's a small safe with its door open – and there's loads of bundles of money set out around it. By this time, C is grabbing handfuls of bundles, and it's not long before we've *all* got some," he says sheepishly.

"So we finally leave the room and lock the door. And then we're standing there – all of us with probably fifty grand in total stashed about us – in our pockets, down our underpants and we look at each other like: 'Okay, so what do we do now then?'

"Someone decided that we should go and see Joey [Davidson, the band's manager at the time] because he'd know what to do so off we all went to his room. We knock on the door, wake him up and tell him, and immediately he's giving everyone a slap and telling us to put it all back because in the morning the police will arrive, look at the guest register, and go straight to see the Scally rock band…"

They both laugh.

"Remember," Neil re-iterates, "This was our first time as proper roadies, so we were saying to each other: 'Is every night going to be like *this*?'"

"Absolutely mad," agrees Cammy.

"The other thing about C was that he just wouldn't pay for petrol, he refused."

So he always made someone else pay?

"NO!" they both jump in to explain. "He just *didn't* pay…"

"We used to get to the petrol station and all lay down in the back of the van," recalls Cammy, "and C would get out and fill up, make like he was going to pay, and then jump back in, gun the engine and we'd speed off."

"It got to the point," says Neil, "Where we had to have a little map of England and we marked off all the petrol stations so we didn't 'hit' the same place twice without knowing!"

Fortunately, amid the mayhem, there was time for some music. Cammy and Neil had maintained their jamming relationship with James Joyce: the three were still playing together at The La's' rehearsal rooms whenever the chance arose.

Neil: "It was a good solid thing that we were developing. Of course, the more the band were away recording or whatever, the more time we had to practice, 'cause there was loads of recording going on at various times – they'd be gone for months sometimes, even when they weren't touring."

Cammy: "It got to the point where we'd really got it together, the sound was really good, and then when The La's came back from wherever they'd been at that time, and I think Lee was a bit impressed. He started to pay attention."

Neil agrees: "It was at that time where Chris [Sharrock] had got off and I think Lee was trying to get more of a grip – take more control to get the music right, and he started hanging around with us more than the band. And then jamming and stuff, he started to say, 'This is what I'm looking for! It should be you two in the band, what do you think?'

"And it was difficult because we knew we were onto a good thing with what we were doing already but... joining The La's meant being signed, doing it all properly, making that next step which was what we'd always hoped for, you know?"

They accepted Mavers' offer, but didn't have any illusions about the state of things within and surrounding the band.

Cammy: "When we joined the band properly, things weren't right really. I think we'd both loved The La's the most in the early days – with Badger, and then Hemmings. Things were going wrong when we joined, no doubt about it. But... [*pauses to think*] it was as much about trying to help Lee get to the right sound as much as it was about anything else, not 'being in the band'."

"And," says Neil, "That's the reason we didn't really do any recording for ages after we joined. The plan was for us to rehearse and get out doing gigs to really get tight as a band – get the sound *right*, and forget about anything else. That's the whole point, after all: to get the vibe right. In the end, I think there was a lot of pressure from the company to get the album done. The magic had been happening before we joined, really. I'd seen the light start to go out of our Lee with all the changes of members and everything."

Relations with Go! Discs remained frosty, Cammy recalls:

"I remember that anything to do with them always seemed to be a problem. For me, I thought that going to see your record company would be a good thing, a nice thing, but, whenever we'd go down to London, it was always a big heavy meeting. It wasn't great, that side of it," he admits.

It would seem that Andy Macdonald was quite patient and put a lot of financial support behind the band, so that must have shown some amount of commitment. Neil disagrees.

"The thing with him was: I don't think he really understood about the music. I think he realised that, with Lee, he had something really, really special but he didn't quite know what to do with him. I think he was probably scared that Lee might go to some other record company if he let him go, and it would all be a big success somewhere else. So he kept on trying and trying, I think is the answer. Hoping it would work out."

Eventually, the issue of the album had to be addressed. The band went into the studio with producer Steve Lillywhite and began the sessions, lasting about three months, which would yield the eventual album.

"I think – no, *I'm sure* – that was the only recording session we ever did," says Neil. "Because we'd spent a long time rehearsing the sound, getting it right, and then it was like all of sudden we had to go and do the record. And it was made clear that this was going to be the last chance for the band. Whatever happened, this was *going* to be the album, so it had better be good."

The sessions were not happy. The band was dissatisfied with the sound, Mavers most of all.

"We had this plan," remembers Neil, "Just to play, well, not our best, hoping maybe that they wouldn't put it out if it wasn't up to scratch."

"We just walked out in the end" is how Cammy describes it.

But Go! Discs were not about to give up. In September of 1990, nearly two years after their last record release (the 'There She Goes' single), a new La's single appeared.

'Timeless Melody' was the first fruit of the collaboration with Lillywhite. Arriving in several brilliantly coloured designs, all formats featured the first use of the notorious La's 'eye' artwork.

To the keen observer, the 'Timeless' release was an indication that all was not well: not one of the B-side tracks had been recorded by the current line-up of the band and nothing appearing there had been recorded within the last twelve months. 'Knock Me Down' was making its second B-side appearance on what was only the band's third single release. 'Over' had been recorded three years earlier while the band rehearsed in Liverpool prior to signing with Go! Discs.[33] The last of the B-sides was 'Clean Prophet' which hailed from the band's time at the Pink Museum studios in Liverpool in 1989.[34]

'Over' is spoken of reverentially by fans and former band members. The generally held view is that this song represents the one time when The La's attempted a song, played it and recorded it once, and were happy with the results.[35]

Considering the circumstances of its recording (dusty old barn, portable tape recorder, quite a lot of 'weed' probably), it all comes off very nicely. The simple, slow-walking minor-chord progression and weary lyrics go together well:

> Over, the storm is over
> Over, it's all blown over...

Hemmings' spacey-sounding echo-drenched electric guitar adds to the dreamy effect and even the half-fluffed ending doesn't seem to matter: the song exists in its own little world.

'Clean Prophet' is another example of Mavers' passion for unusual time signatures. The jarring staccato guitar-strumming on this track grabs the listener from the off. Mavers seems to be talking in semi-autobiographical terms:

> Wild eyes, realise this eager dream to prophesise
> Ev'rybody's got a dream, show them what you mean

At one point, the band seems to be drifting into The Kinks' 'Sunny Afternoon' ("Take me, take me, take me by the hand I cannot see...")

The guitar solo (presumably played by Sutton) seems deliberately maniacal. Off-kilter whistling can be heard amid evil-sounding background laughter. The brevity of the song is emphasised by its neatly abrupt ending.

"I don't even know if we were told it was coming out," recalls Neil of the 'Timeless' single release. "Maybe Lee was. There wasn't anything in the way of consultation with the label – Lee would've said no anyway.

"Even the video was just put together from bits of live shows – odds and ends."

The accompanying video for the song did indeed seem to be a grab-bag of straight-ahead live footage interspersed with one or two clever animated segments, which featured The La's name magically appearing in sand and tiny animated cave-drawing men coming to life. The single clocked up just two weeks on the charts and reached number fifty-seven, an improvement of two places upon the last single, 'There She Goes'.

But The La's themselves were not interested. Following the breakdown of the final album sessions, they had returned to Liverpool, leaving Go! Discs and Steve Lillywhite to assemble the album from the hours of tape they had left behind them.

Barry Sutton had recalled: "I'd heard that, in the end, after all the different studios and all the different sessions and producers, the album had costed a million pounds to make."

When the eponymous album was finally released in November of 1990, it arrived with more of a whimper than a bang. Although greeted enthusiastically by the music press, its public reception was lukewarm, at best. The stop-start nature of their musical career meant that The La's' fanbase was devoted, but fractured and fairly small. The album would do only modest business.

By now, this was just what the band (or Mavers at least) wanted. Sent to promote the record by Go! Discs, they seized every opportunity to let the whole world know how they felt. The message came through loud and clear: we hate our record, please don't buy it. It was repeated to any and all available journalists. An interview even appeared in the pre-teen magazine *Smash Hits* ("We hate the album, it never captured anything that we were about") which hardly spoke to the band's audience. They made it plain to the interviewer that they didn't really want to be interviewed and they didn't want their pictures taken. Feelings were being made clear in no uncertain terms.

Things had obviously come to some sort of head by the time a feature appeared in the December 1990 issue of the mainstream and high-profile *Q* magazine. The interview with the band at the rehearsal rooms in Liverpool began with the now-obligatory spleen-venting (by you know who): "All our songs are great, la, but how would you know it when the record's done so badly?

"We thought we'd record it [the album] in about a week, but it didn't turn out like that did it? I don't know why we didn't get our sound, seven different studios at about £1,000-a-day. It's our problem but it's not our fault – it's up to the sound engineers to capture it, the so-called producers… but at the end of the day it's *our name* that goes on the record."

It ends with Mavers commenting sourly: "All this power and shit. And greed… I'd rather be skint and doing what I wanted than not be able to do what I want."

No one actually says, "It's all Go! Discs fault!" But the band's feelings are clear.[36] Perhaps sensing this, *Q* sought out and obtained a very rare (and brief) interview with label head Andy MacDonald. Although not the dirt-throwing response the magazine might have wanted, MacDonald clearly felt a need to put his side of the story. His tone is weary but diplomatic. He confesses that the label/band relationship is "not all it needs to be" but professes to like the album:

"It's the best version so far. We think it's a great record – Lee's very talented but he can't recognise how good the record really is. Steve Lillywhite did a brilliant job in difficult circumstances and, if he hadn't been as patient as he was, it's doubtful the record would ever have appeared."

He offers a telling perspective on Mavers' 'artistic' temperament: "You know, John Lennon hated the recording of 'Strawberry Fields Forever' till the day he died…"

So, is the album actually as good as MacDonald thought or as bad as

Mavers told the press it was?

The answer probably lies somewhere between. What's plain is that artist and label had very different agendas.

Opening the album is 'Son of a Gun', a song frequently used to open shows. Most bands' first albums lean heavily on their live repertoire: the songs are well-rehearsed and represent most of the original material available to them at that time. It seems that Lillywhite (and Mavers, *if* he was involved in the production and track-selection process, which seems unlikely) opted for a straight transfer of The La's' set onto record, pretty much in the order the band had been playing them.

'Son of a Gun' is a natural opener: the Latin-style rhythm fuelled by the acoustic guitar backing grabs the ear straightaway. Although the singing highlights Mavers' high falsetto, the vocals are clearly on the weak side compared to other performances.[37] On this track, one of the oldest songs, Mavers' accent cuts through.

Many commentators have noted the autobiographical allusions in the lyric:

> There was once a boy of life, who lived upon a knife
> He took his share out everywhere, but he never took a wife
> He was burned by the twentieth century
> Now he's doing time in the back of his mind

The track has no sooner faded than 'I Can't Sleep' crashes in and things start to dip. Often one of the final songs in the live set, it has been stripped of most of its power thanks to another tired-sounding Mavers vocal and guitars which sound extremely tinny. Even so, it's interesting to note how tight the band sound. The lyric seems to be a stream-of-consciousness: Mavers sings of strange visions ("There's a big black train/cloud/car coming"). If insomnia is the subject, the feel is well captured by the insistent distorted guitar riffs.[38]

'Timeless Melody' comes next. It's one of Mavers' most explicitly autobiographical songs, tackling the subject of inspiration itself:

> The Melody always finds me
> Whenever the thought reminds me
> Breaking a chain inside my head

Mavers addresses his own apparent inability to express himself:

> Even the words they fail me

> Oh, look what it's doing to me
> I never say what I want to say

The song turns on the phrase "Open your mind". It seems to have been considered an 'important' track (it had, of course, been the 'taster' single prior to the album's release) and was therefore subjected to an 'epic' treatment at odds with the band's musical style. The tempo drags – as though the whole band want to play the song faster than they actually are doing (certainly, it is usually played a lot faster on live recordings). Numerous overdubs pop in and out, unwelcomely, during the track. Things are lifted briefly by a wonderfully brittle guitar solo from Cammy, but it is a highlight in an otherwise washed-out take of what should be a key La's track.

By contrast, the next song, 'Liberty Ship', gives an indication of how things should have been. Never much more than a diverting ditty built around a shuffling guitar riff, the irony is that, on something relatively throwaway, everyone shines. Lillywhite gets it spot-on. Power's bass bumps along as if possessed by the spirits of Stanley Clarke and Paul McCartney combined. Whether or not his lines were dictated by Mavers (and they probably were), his playing sparkles. The track is lifted no end by some sensitive mixing, letting the acoustic guitars and bass drift in and out. Brilliantly off-kilter but indispensable is the acoustic guitar break (played by Cammy?).

For a moment, we are transported to the rehearsal rooms back in Liverpool as Mavers rallies the band with his lyrics of self-sacrifice:

> I am the sailor, the ocean slave
> Fill your sail with the breath I gave
> And this I gave for all mankind
> Sail away on the ocean wave…

As the final line "Sail away on the ocean wave" becomes "Sail away on the air waves", the track fades – all too quickly. Then we're treated to the re-mixed 'There She Goes'. Why the decision to remix the original 1988 version was taken remains a mystery – perhaps Mavers, apparently unhappy with that mix, wanted another go; perhaps Lillywhite did. Whatever the reason, it is the proverbial broth which should have been left unspoiled. Stripped of almost all the vocal harmonies and sweeping bottom bass end on the original, the song is given a wind-tunnel feel with Mavers' vocal often getting lost in the roar. In truth, it's not possible to ruin the song completely – it's simply too good – but the contrast between the two versions could hardly be greater.[39]

After the relative high of 'Liberty Ship' and 'There She Goes', things reach a low point with 'Doledrum'. Possessed of the most tired-sounding Mavers vocal on the album with backing vocals that sound like they were canned and processed before they even got into the studio, it is entirely at odds with the song's ethos. (To be 'in the doledrums' being a northern England expression to mean being fed up.) Far from not going down to Doledrum, Mavers sounds like he's already there: "Oh no, don't go down to doledrum."

Even with 'Callin' All' left off the album, it's surprising that tracks like 'Doledrum' and 'Freedom Song' made the final list when there was much stronger B-side material available (viz: 'Who Knows?' and 'All By Myself').

After the downbeat 'Doledrum' (which ended the first side of the vinyl format) comes 'Feelin''. Being one of the oldest amongst all old (by then) songs, it sounds simply too polished, too smooth – if ever there was a La's track to be brought in 'warts and all', it would have been this one.[40]

'Way Out', previously released as a single, is next. The track has been completely re-recorded from the original acoustic guitar-driven version to a re-vamped electric (and faster) beast. And... it works, again largely due to the extremely tight playing of the band.

Apart from the great songwriting on display, the other important ingredient in The La's album is the variety of rhythms used throughout the twelve songs. Mavers is clearly at home in almost any style: waltz ('Way Out'), Latin tempos ('Son of a Gun' and, although not on the album, 'Come In, Come Out') and even the hardest of all tempos to write in, the march ('Freedom Song'). And the album is peppered with his imaginative rhythm guitar playing, often tucked unobtrusively into the mix.

A case in point is the next track, 'IOU'. There is an astonishing dexterity to the acoustic guitar riffs that can be heard during the verses: some of the string bends have an intensity that sounds like the lower strings being pulled off the guitar. The song somehow mixes the idea of a debt (an "IOU") and themes of oneness and mutual dependency:

> I'll feed you, you'll feed me
> I'll see you can stand on your own two feet

And then the inspired middle section:

> On the farm, linking you arm in arm
> There's no harm, in greasing your neighbour's palm...

The odd man out on such a varied album is 'Freedom Song'. Set in a strange tempo (see above), it sounds as though it exists in an entirely new musical key. Bleak lyrics alluding to weaponry, bombs and warfare turn almost vaudevillian-sounding when Mavers launches into:

> I'm not scared to die, God help me
> We went to the same schools and we
> All learned the same rules of lament

You can almost see Mavers strolling centre-stage in some dusty old theatre during some imagined musical and singing those lines. The simple structure of the song belies the lyrical flourishes – "rules of lament"? And the wonderful: "Accidents show mercy none". (Chernobyl anyone?)

After the faltering grace of that track, we are given Mavers' answer to Dylan's 'Subterranean Homesick Blues', 'Failure'.

In a cascade of seemingly unconnected lyrics and imagery over loud, trashy, distorted backing, Mavers treats us to his own personal, youthful hell-at-home-domestic-boredom insanity. The sound of the track might strike the listener as a little dated now but it's worth bearing in mind that, at the time of the album's release, the word 'grunge' had still to be coined. That music itself was unheard outside of downtown Seattle.

This is Mavers' own homegrown rockabilly-Mersey-proto-grunge – and it's taking no prisoners. Right from the start, the wailing feedback and chord-vamping guitar riff sets the tone as Mavers' to-the-limit vocal delivers the lines. In setting out his stir-crazy circumstances, there is an undercurrent of humour but the end is bleak:

> So you open the door with a look on your face
> With your hands in your pockets and your family to face
> And you go downstairs and you sit in your place...

Throughout the track Power, Neil Mavers and Cammy pile on the pressure, right through to the briefly reprised ending. Their playing is fluid and perfectly timed – surely the result of playing the song many, many times.

Finally, we come to 'Looking Glass': if 'There She Goes' is the romantic heart of The La's' music, 'Looking Glass' is undoubtedly its tortured but beautiful soul. In it, Mavers seems to crystallize his concept of 'oneness' and brotherhood of humanity and the ongoing cycle of, well, everything. His voice is never more affecting than at the start of this song as he sings:

Oh tell me where I'm going
Tell me where I'm bound...
Turn the pages over
Turn the world around...

The tension slowly builds, the key almost imperceptibly changes from major to minor ("*turn* the world around...") and the guitar picks out the chorus melody:

I've seen everybody
Everybody's seen me
In the looking glass...

Again Mavers mines the modal scales to give his song an epic feel. The main melody, built upon a revolving cycle of three chords, sounds almost eastern and raga-like.

Like a giant musical orgasm, the sound builds and builds as the chorus repeats again and again until, about halfway through ("The glass is *smashed*..."[41]), the whole band shifts up a gear, slowly increasing the tempo. Deep in the mix, we can hear Mavers reaching all sorts of high harmony notes with his falsetto. Bubbling under in the mix, lines from other songs drift in and out as all The La's' music merges.[42] Mavers leads the band on in a shaman-like repeat of the three key chords. Finally, when Neil Mavers and Cammy can drum and strum no faster, it all ends in a cacophony of musical collapse. There is no final crashing chord *à la* 'A Day In The Life', just the dying feedback from thrashed-out guitars.

'Looking Glass' fares better than most of the songs on the album, precisely because it is the kind of song which calls for a kind of 'epic' treatment, and Lillywhite goes some way to redeeming himself by trying to enhance the already clearly magnificent. Not one member of the band puts a foot wrong musically, even when the tempo becomes intolerably high.

Now that the dust of over a decade has settled on *The La's*, how does it shine?

The timing of the album's release is an historical irony. Had it been successfully recorded and released within the usual timescale, the album would long since have secured its place as the definitive start of the pop guitar band revival. It would've been on the shelves a good six or nine months before the Stone Roses seminal debut, released in May 1989. As it was, *The La's* arrived towards the messy end of the Madchester phase some eighteen months later, only a few months apart from The Happy Mondays' *Pills Thrills & Bellyaches* behemoth album.

It is not inconceivable that an earlier release might have radically altered the course of the Baggy movement, shaming the numerous Roses copyists into ditching their bell-bottoms and wah-wah pedals and coming up with more original, trad-style songs. A Britpop revolution in 1988?

Responses to the album today invariably remark upon the 'freshness' of the songs, noting that the album sounds as if it could've been released relatively recently, that it wears its twelve-year vintage well. To an extent, this reflects the stagnation of many of the mainstream bands post-Britpop. More importantly, it highlights *The La's'* ambitious agenda, the musical territory which it stakes out.

The record is, as much as anything, a blueprint for 'the modern band record', touching as it does on many now-staple themes, while simultaneously avoiding overt romanticism ('There She Goes' being the only ostensible 'love' song in sight and that lyric doesn't even employ the word). Issues of state of mind, feelings of displacement, inspiration, boredom and escape are beguilingly interwoven with a set of imaginatively constructed songs. The mixture of genres Mavers draws on – folk, rockabilly, grunge-style (as it would now be recognised), country and lightweight psychedelia and punk among others – gently but consistently wrong-foots the listener in the rare but pleasurable way that only a really original record can. Issues of production aside[43], Mavers' masterplan shines through for the discerning, committed listener.

The whispered promise of the album is its final trump card: 'You like this?' it says, 'Well, imagine how much better the definitive article might have been.'

The mistake that many commentators past and present have made is to rely too heavily on allusions to the Sixties feel of the songs/album. While Mavers is clearly a fan of older and simpler recording methods and often spoke passionately about Sixties figures, his music is by no means anachronistic. The presentation of the material sometimes suggests otherwise but the songs' content could hardly be more contemporary.

This uncanny resonance makes Mavers' continuing absence all the more alluring to the curious: the songs' manner echoes major musical figures of the recent past. Triumphant chest-beating inspiration? Oasis. High-voltage passion and musical/spiritual aspiration? The Verve. Confused isolation and weariness? Radiohead, natch.

Mavers, as The La's – and the supplemental B-side material – reminds us, had the ground staked out before making his unscheduled exit stage left.

While Mavers' struggle to crystallise his vision will always be an element of the listening experience of *The La's*, tales of his frustration should not obscure what he achieved. Flawed as it is, the album remains a touchstone for the modern songwriter. As history has shown, it is the songs themselves that survive. It is the songs which have the capacity for a peculiar kind of longevity and rebirth which can wash away the baggage, and leave the essence. Which can then be judged on its own terms.

Despite the band's unwillingness to endorse the album's release, it seemed that the world was finally ready for The La's in late 1990. The re-released 'There She Goes' was climbing the UK charts as the album was released and would reach a very rewarding number five, staying on the charts for a total of nine weeks. There was a solid live appearance by the band performing the song at the Liverpool Albert Docks which was broadcast on *Top Of The Pops*. The Steve Lillywhite remix had replaced the original version of the song, of course, but the record-buying public didn't seem to mind.

B-sides for the release were the shortly-to-be-heard-on-the-album 'Freedom Song' and another track, 'All By Myself.'

This last song hails from the Pink Museum sessions which yielded 'Clean Prophet' and bears absolutely no relation to Eric Carmen's 1970s Rachmaninov-inspired slush ballad of the same name. A Mavers original and the definitive testament to the quality of La's B-sides, 'All By Myself' is truly the Great Lost La's Song. Apart from some distant harmonies and slight bass guitar, the track is virtually a solo performance. A song with depth and despair in equal measure, it is not a 'happy' listen – such is its understated power, it would not have seem out of place on a Nick Drake record.[44]

While there may be speculation over Mavers' guitar technique, his playing here is both at once intricate and beautifully executed.[45] The richness and intimacy of the recording is very akin to 'Who Knows', but the material much bleaker. There is no salvation in sight for Mavers here as he delivers some of his best lyrics:

> All by myself, I will chase away the sickness, all by myself
> All by myself, I will pray for my forgiveness, all by myself...

It's hard not to be touched by such heartfelt sentiment. The sense of isolation and hopelessness is palpable. One can only wonder at the decision to leave this song off the album. What other gems from the 'Pink' sessions – or indeed other sessions – remain unheard, deep in the vaults of

Go! Discs?

When the band took to the road to promote the album, the live reviews were generally ecstatic and acknowledged the fact that Mavers had 'taken time' to get things right.

During 1991, the band turned in a blistering live set for Radio One's *Evening Session* which went some way to demonstrating what the long-awaited album had failed to catch. The synchronicity of the band is jaw-dropping as they blast through definitive versions of 'I Can't Sleep', 'Timeless Melody' (a slower, more powerful version), 'Callin' All' and a truly superb version of 'Feelin'', played at top speed with Mavers beating out the intro rhythm on his guitar and shouting out the count-in excitedly at the start. It's clear that this final, solid line-up was probably the definitive incarnation of The La's and perhaps as close as Mavers ever got to achieving his ideal sound.

Following the release of the band's last single, 'Feelin'', in 1991,[46] they toured Europe, and then the US and Middle East, all under the auspices of supporting the album.

"It was just a chance to get out and have some fun, maybe try to recapture some of the inspiration, you know? We hoped that maybe different places and different people would just bring some of it all back," says Neil.

"But," says Cammy, "There was also a part of it being that we had to pay the debt back, just to generate some money for the label – and us. The plan had changed a bit, because we'd done all the studios and stuff and now we were thinking about kitting out the rehearsal room to record."

"There was even the thought," recalls Neil, "that once all the album stuff had died down, we might have been able to talk the label round to our way of thinking. They weren't going to drop us, so it seemed like it was maybe a matter of staying with the devil you know and working it out. And they did give a bit more each time, or it seemed they did.

"But, in the end," says Neil, "It just seemed like a lost cause."

One of Power's last appearances with the band was with Mavers and a couple of pick-up musicians performing 'There She Goes' on America's famous *David Letterman Show*, the last gasp of the small attempt to get the band noticed over there following the album release.

We talk about Power's departure from the band.

"I think there were two camps in the band by that time," remembers Cammy, "And John was coming out with a few songs, which I think expressed his situation, how he was feeling. I don't think that they were directed *at* Lee particularly, but he [Power] obviously wasn't happy."

"Yeah," says Neil, "It was never: this is a song about you and I'm going to sing it *at* you, not at all. It was just the time, I think, the circumstances, and looking back *now* maybe you can see a bit more, read a bit more into it. I don't know. Lee and John had gone through a lot, and I don't think it was a surprise when he left."

"But even when he was gone," says Cammy, "There was no time off. We were down the practice room almost every night…"

"Things were starting to fall to bits then, though," Neil recalls. "Joycer [James Joyce] came in for a bit, did a few gigs, and then it was dribs and drabs of things, gigs, rehearsing. The whole thing was just grinding to a halt. A terrible time."

"We did those few gigs in the mid-Nineties, whenever it was, but there wasn't any… we knew things weren't in any fit state. There was no manager then, we just rang places up and asked if we could have a gig…"[47]

Neil continues the story, after he and Cammy had left.

"It went quiet after we got off, and Lee eventually started to do a little bit down in a studio in London at Kew Bridge, and Andy Macdonald was backing him, and saying he could do it all just as he wanted to. So I went down after a bit and we were just messing for a while and then it got a bit more serious and it lasted about a year, just rehearsing in the studio. It was me and Lee and Edgar Summertyme and Lee Garnet, who was a lad who'd been around for a while visiting and played some basic guitar. And Lee was getting bits for himself to help him record – he got his recording desk and stuff.

"But it still wasn't a great feeling because of all the problems there'd been in the past. We *wanted* it to be there, but it wasn't, and that's when Lee knocked it on the head and said he'd had enough for good.

"Now," says Neil, "We've got something which is a lot better than The La's *for us*. Don't get me wrong, we loved The La's, loved them, but this is just better for us. With hindsight, maybe we should have just kept going as we were at the start and who knows where we would have been now?" He laughs.

"The thing with Lee," opines Cammy, "is that he can get a great-sounding chord, give it a brilliant rhythm and then stick an even better melody line on top. And he can do it at the drop of a hat, and I've seen him do it time and time again.

"It's just a shame that he's encountered so much trouble trying to get it together with his music. I wish he could just get a little something together and not worry about it too much and let the songs come out and *give* to people a little of what he's got, because it's so great, you know?"

It's all over too quickly and we're walking back to Cammy's car. At this point, Neil feels he has spotted a flaw in my approach.

"It seems that you're focusing on a lot of the bad stuff – you know, the problems with the album and the label. You need to make the point that, yeah, there was that, but there were also a lot of great, great times which we all had. A lot of very inspiring music, friendships. It was like a big adventure when you look back on it now. You need to make that clear, it's important."

It is.

Chapter Eight
The Enthusiast

"A man can only attain knowledge with the help of those who possess it. One must learn from him who knows" – George Gurdjieff

"One of the ultimate advantages of an education is simply coming to the end of it" – Prof. B F Skinner

I would be a liar if I said that I'd planned exactly how all this would come together, but two thoughts *were* in my mind when I sat down to try to write the story of The La's: firstly, it would be very unlikely that Mavers would talk to me. I would just have to accept that and work around it as best as I could.

The second thought was that, at some point, I would need to talk to John Power and that it would be difficult, probably the biggest challenge of all.

Writing the book without input from Mavers was one thing – after all, his very reputation would lead people to expect that he hadn't co-operated. It was practically a given. But John Power was a different matter. Next to Mavers, no one is more bound up in the story of The La's. Therefore it followed that few others' input would be as important.

Having left The La's to form Cast, who then went on to have the fastest and biggest-selling debut album in the history of the Polydor record label [several million copies sold], it was clear from the outset that the old tried-and-tested get-the-number-and-ring-them-up-out-of-the-blue-and-ask-if-they-want-to-talk-about-The-La's formula just wasn't going to work. In short, we're talking about the big time now (or as big as the 'big time' in The La's story gets, anyway) and I'm definitely out of my depth.

Yet how could I complete the book without speaking to Power?

Interviews he had done about The La's following his departure made it fairly clear (at least to me, reading between the lines) that he didn't really want to dwell on the past and wasn't especially inclined these days to discuss his time with the band and Mavers.

I deal with the problem initially by not dealing with it. There is so much else going on and so many other people to talk to that I decide to leave any thoughts of contacting Power until later on – I figure that the more people I've spoken to, the more seriously I will be taken when I do eventually try.

'Later on' inevitably arrives – at a point when I've spoken to almost every source I can and written a large amount of the book.

Power's manager is also involved in the story of The La's so I hope to kill two birds with one stone.

After sending some draft chapters to his management and making numerous unreturned telephone calls, I am eventually told that neither Power nor his management are willing to be interviewed.

It's definitely a setback. For some reason I had assumed that Power would want to talk. Now that he doesn't, I'm not quite sure where it leaves me. For a while I'm crestfallen (maybe they thought what I'd written wasn't very good?).

In the end, though, I'm not giving up and resolve to examine the sources and material already available from older interviews and see what can be made from those.

It might be an obvious point to make but there is no doubt that John Power – and specifically his relationship with Mavers – was one of the key elements of The La's.

Power's survival in a group where others came and went is testament to his and Mavers' musical (and, no doubt, general) compatibility. It is almost certainly true, too, that the band might not have lasted as long as they did as a working musical entity, continually trying to capture the right sound, without Power's enthusiasm and support.

In a way, his role in the group seems in part to have been to be a friendlier, more accessible version of Lee Mavers. Where Mavers was often intense and serious to the point of sometimes seeming uncommunicative and 'difficult', Power seemed to be tarred with the same brush but in lighter shades. It was often Power who spoke to the audiences at gigs, Power who took the lead in interviews as much as Mavers did. Behind the scenes, what had started as a teacher/pupil relationship blossomed into something more even-footed during the six or so years Power was in the band. Ironically, it was this transition which would eventually cause him to leave.

Speaking to the music press in the mid-Nineties, several years after leaving the band, Power reminisced: "It was an adventure. In the early days me and Lee were close, and it was exciting because no one else knew us. The La's were full of great dreams and, from Day One, we knew we were the best fucking band kicking around.

"It was a razor-edge feeling we all had, we knew what we wanted...

"But you have to remember, I was young, la, only nineteen. My mates tell me now that I was a nutter – just shouting and enthusin' and going off my head!!"

It was this enthusiasm, though, as Mike Badger had recalled, which was what Mavers and he needed as much as anything during those early days of 1986. Simple but solid bass lines, a passion for 'weed' and a good sense of humour were the prerequisites. Also, though, someone who was happy to be musically subservient to Mavers and follow his lead.

In a later interview Power talked about the formation of his relationship with Mavers:

"We got on straightaway – it was all very natural, it was weird. Mike [Badger], Lee and myself: it just felt like part of the plan. I can't explain it to you. If you believe in the future and something that's brewing in you, then finding people like that is just great. I learned to play in that environment – I wasn't a player who joined the band, I was just a lad with enthusiasm. They recognised it in my eyes. They must have thought: 'Well, he's got everything apart from the fact that he's never played bass in his life.'

"It wasn't just an attitude, it was like I knew the power of music more than anyone. Apart from Lee, of course...

"The first La's following was basically about forty of my mates. I still had this big crew, so I'd phone them up and it was, like, 'I'm fucking playing a gig!' and they were like: 'Wha?!' It was real news, one of the lads being in a band."

And so it began. After Badger's departure, drummers and guitarists came and went but Mavers and Power, like some endlessly re-combining chemical, remained the core. It was their relationship (guitar and bass) which allowed the band to continue to function when others left. At no time did Mavers ever have to re-invent the group from scratch by himself. In the same way that the bass guitar underpins the whole sound of a modern band, so their relationship underpinned The La's. Power was content for Mavers to take the lead musically as he practised his playing. Even when the endless quest for the right recording of the album started, Power sat back and said nothing, despite reservations which he revealed only after leaving the group:

"When we started going into the studio, I was a bit suspicious because Lee wanted to do all the recording in the kitchen. And it was like: 'Nah, that sounds wrong' and 'Don't dust the guitars – they sound better with the dust on them.' So I realised all was not right..."

Speaking to Q magazine around the same time as this, he confirmed his views about which version of The La's album was the best:

"The best recordings we did were with Mike Hedges because he'd got an old Abbey Road Studio Two desk.[48] The version of the album done on that was amazing. Lee was kissing everyone going: 'That's it! That's it! We've done it!' And it did seem like that. It was the third proper attempt so we were all relieved."

However, those recordings were scrapped[49] and things began to take a turn for the worse. And yet Power stuck with it (and Mavers) after his favourite recordings of the band were discarded and further periods in the wilderness beckoned.

But a change was coming for the Mavers/Power relationship and, ironically enough, it was music which would be the cause. Power had been given a co-writing credit on the song 'Over', which had been recorded in 1987 prior to the band signing to Go! Discs, but, at the turn of the new decade, he began to make his own small, slow forays into songwriting proper. How was Mavers to deal with this change in the dynamic of the band and his relationship with Power? The pupil was now moving more towards the position of equal, no longer simply content to be 'the bass player'.

The split with Mike Badger had clearly shown who was musically in charge of The La's. Since then, only Mavers' songs had been played by the band. It's hard to imagine other band members being given a chance to play their material (if they had any) by Mavers – given the history of the group and Mavers' own reputation for control, they would no doubt have been too sheepish. But Power's emerging material was a different matter. Because of the longstanding friendship between the two of them, it wouldn't be possible for Mavers to dismiss it out of hand if he didn't like it, and yet up to that point The La's had been, musically, his sole property. Would he retain musical control but risk isolating himself from Power?

In the end, it seems that a compromise was reached whereby Power's songs would be included in the live set, and he would also get to sing them. Not that there were that many to be included. At this stage, Power had only a couple of songs anyway: 'Fly On' (know later as 'Alright') and 'Follow Me Down'.

Power: "I was coming into a bubble as a writer. I had these little tunes – I wasn't really capable of working on them. It was clear that I was more interested in my own stuff than anyone else's..."

But no Power songs were ever to be released under the banner of The La's. There never was much chance of them being chosen as singles – but none of his songs were featured on the eventual album nor the B-sides of the singles released around that time (the re-release of 'There She Goes', 'Timeless Melody' and, finally, 'Feelin').

As the prospect of further La's releases began to seem ever more distant, so too did any possibility of Power's songs seeing the light of day.

And the compromise reached was under strain. Power's songs began to be an apparent source of tension for the band, certainly for Mavers and Power themselves. While Power always sang the backing vocals for all The La's songs live, it seems Mavers grew unwilling to return the favour. Things had clearly come to a head by the time of the London Town and Country gig in 1990. The band was supposedly promoting the release of Go! Discs' version of the album, but the stage was becoming a battleground for the clashing of egos.

No more the reticent pupil when it came to his own music, a tape of the gig reveals a frustrated Power changing the lyrics to the chorus of 'Follow Me Down' from "Won't you follow me down?" to "Won't you sing the backing vocals?"

The song ends fairly abruptly and there's clearly some sort of altercation going on.[50] It ends with Power telling the audience: "We like each other really..." but with a notable lack of conviction.

He recalled the incident in interview several years later:

"We'd just started and, second song in, it was guitars down and head-to-head between me and Lee. It was always, you know, 'if you're not going to sing on my song, I'm not going to sing on your fucking song.' Just stupid schoolyard stuff. We'd put a new song of mine into the set and he'd decided, because it was my song, he wasn't going to sing. So I started shouting at him and we stopped and it all went off..."

In Power's own words just at the time of release of Cast's debut album:

"Towards the end of my time in The La's, I thought I had to get something together. Basically, there were two bands in one band. There aren't many nice memories..."

The ill-conceived US and Middle Eastern La's tour of mid-1991 found a weary Power still toeing the party line but with an indication of what was to come.

He told NME, who were with the band in the States at the time: "It's a bit of a blur. It's the longest tour we've ever done... six weeks is probably average for everyone else but for us to get our act together for six weeks is something else, la."

The article is interesting because it demonstrates Power's importance to the group PR-wise. Mavers barely says two words to the interviewer. It's left to Power to build bridges and give the music press what they want.

The talk turned to recording:

"Hopefully, we know what we want in the studio. You learn from your past, like – we want to produce it. We want to get a true representation of the band down on record. There's loads of new stuff, la, stuff we've never even done live, which is going to make it more exciting for us. Lee's got loads of tunes, and this last year-and-a-half has been fucking brilliant for me for writing. I reckon I could make a living making melodies... me Dad always said there's a great living to be had there..."

After he had left the group, Power could be by turns both dismissive and respectful of his time in the band. On the one hand:

"Personally, in The La's I was just playing bass. Only now am I getting to perform my songs properly, and only now do I believe in them. Back then, the whole thing wasn't right."

And: "I don't really give a shit what Lee thinks [about Cast]. Really don't give two flying fucks to be honest. That's not nasty: I just stopped worrying about what he thought when I left the fucking band. I couldn't be arsed spending eight years in the studio and then scrapping it, but I've heard the songs he's got and they're great, so it's up to him."

And most dismissively: "The La's are the past, and they were only important to a little group of Scallies. Cast mean a lot more to me."

These quotes are drawn from early in Cast's career. As the years have passed, Power seems to have grown more philosophical. Talking near the end of the 1990s, he was far more positive:

"Lee had a strong influence on me, oh yeah. When it came to conversations with him, it was good. Of course, it was very inspirational for me. It all just flows into the stream, like.

"It wasn't bad, no. Things happen in life which are bad, but The La's were good – I just left. I didn't have to ask someone if my songs were good, it was just a progression. I was becoming a songwriter and you either react to things or you don't.

"I was just feeling uninspired. I left to do my own stuff... somewhere along the line you have to make your own decisions about what you want to do in life. We'd come back from Japan and America and I just wanted to put some new songs in the set. I'd been playing the same fucking songs for six-and-a-half years and I said to myself: 'I'm not playing them again.' I had three new songs which I thought were good.[51] I felt that, if I didn't try them then, no one would ever know. I'd just be fucking bitter the rest of my life.

"Cast existed from the day I left The La's, but all I had were the songs and my belief in them."

As one music journalist noted at the time of release of the first Cast album, being in The La's should have equipped John Power for absolutely nothing. And yet, as Mike Badger had commented, what an education it would be for anyone to spend such a period of time with Mavers. While it's true that many musicians are frustrated writers, few ever take the steps to fulfill their potential. John Power went from being a skinny eighteen-year-old mad pot-head with no musical ability to the singer and songwriter in one of the leading British bands of the mid-1990s. The link between the two? Undoubtedly, the influence of Lee Mavers.

As John Byrne had noted:

"John was always willing to learn and trying to study things, he was always asking about middle-eights and keys and things like that. You could see the enthusiasm he had."

Although warmly received by the music press (at a time when virtually any new band was warmly received), Cast never quite attained the critical respect that Mavers and The La's did. The NME dubbed their debut album a "triumph of application over inspiration" and several commentators noted that Power had left The La's only to re-invent his own watered-down version of them in which he played the 'Mavers role' himself (guitar and vocals and performing only his songs).

Others continued to draw out the Mavers/Powers 'mind games' theory by drawing allusions from Cast's lyrics which, they claimed, reflected Power's feelings about his old friend:

> Do you think I miss you?
> Do you think I care?
> Did you think I'd lay down and die?[52]
> From the back of my mind I still see you
> Still believe in you[53]

Still, Power was plagued by links to his old cohort, as he commented in one interview:

"Someone picked up on the fact that 'Cast' is the last word on the last song on The La's album. That's a strange co-incidence, don't you think?"

"I don't see Lee. The last time was probably walking down the road. He's a funny... I leave it to people. You know, I leave people to their own devices..."

Chapter Nine
Failure

"What keeps the boat up? Will." – Lee Mavers, NME *interview 1991*

"There's a popular idea that the flirtation with chaos is something you must grow out of but I believe that, while you shouldn't hang to your adolescence like it was a state of grace, you should leave yourself the latitude to go berserk from time to time" – from *'Growing Up True Is Hard To Do',* Lester Bangs, *1978*

"Nothing was ever said, but we had a few jams and I knew I was in…"

I find James Joyce at the top of a tower block in Huyton, practicing his bass guitar with a tiny amplifier.

In the New Year of 1992, following the departure of John Power, what remained of The La's (Mavers, brother Neil and Cammy) assembled at the band's rehearsal rooms in Liverpool for what was probably the beginning of the lowest point in the group's story. Even if Mavers had seen it coming, Power leaving would have been a blow to morale, if only because he had been such a constant for so long. That, coupled with their isolation from Go! Discs, certainly made it seem likely that the end was now nigh, even for come-back kid extraordinaire Mavers.

While cannabis (weed) and the like had always been a part of The La's' musical and social world[54], drugs, and particularly hard drugs, were now beginning to tighten their grip on the inner circle of the band. Outside, a world which had barely got to know them was already beginning to forget.

There was, though, a plan. Of sorts. It was the same plan Mavers had had for the past eight-ish years: play music. Play music whatever happens. Sporadic jamming and practising continued, but with a vacant bass-playing slot.

Neil Mavers and Cammy had been playing together as a threesome with bassist James Joyce, cribbing practice time at The La's' rehearsal rooms when the call came for the first two to become full-time band members.[55] This left Joyce high-and-dry. He drifted away from the band's circle of friends and had taken a regular job when a chance meeting with Cammy led him back to the practice room, Mavers, and the bass guitar slot left vacant by John Power.

Joyce recalls that Power later turned up at the first post-Power La's gig but he sensed the frosty atmosphere between Mavers and his old sidekick:

"It was obvious that John and Lee had been mates from way back but, to see them together at that time, there wasn't much there to be honest, or there didn't seem to be."

Rehearsals continued with Joyce on board. He admits that, even with Power gone, there was still a lot of tension within the band.

"Tension. Definitely. There was a lot of repetition – Lee would drive you through the same songs again and again at the rehearsals, the same set in the same order. You did end up feeling that you were a shit musician and people were really paranoid about being sacked from the band."

Joyce, barely at the end of his teens, had worshipped The La's from afar and was keen to please: "I bent over backwards to stay in the band really, and that did lead me to do some things I now regret. But I was young and I loved The La's, the music of The La's, the *idea* of The La's, worshipped the ground they walked on really, and I just wanted to be a part of it."

He is perhaps a bit over-humble about his time in the band.

"Mainly, you know, I just filled in really – what with John having gone and everything, you know, those dates which they had to play. But the rot had set in, no doubt at all."

With outstanding live commitments met, the group settled back into their rehearsal rooms where Joyce was to become a first-hand witness to Mavers' desire to experiment with sound and music.

"Mad things, honest to god. I remember one time that he [Mavers] was getting us to tune into feedback coming from the amps. Tuning into feedback! It sounds mad now, but Lee always managed to explain things in such a way that you ended up feeling that it *could* actually be done.[56] You were ready to do the impossible: 'We can do it!' You could see that he was inspired but his mind was going elsewhere, in other directions…"

The rehearsals continued their tense run. Joyce recalls Mavers paying particular attention to his brother:

"Lee really came down hard on Neil, really hard. It might have been a 'brothers' thing but… as far as I was concerned, Neil was – and is – a brilliant drummer, he's just got such great swing. But Lee was having none of that, you know – Neil was a 'millionth' out or whatever, and Lee wasn't having it *at all* until everything was perfect.

"They came to blows on a few occasions. It was a stressful time. I remember Lee had just had his first son and had just bought his house and so there was all sorts of pressure…"

Joyce, young and keen but also coming back into the band's circle from the outside, could see what was happening:

"It was just all falling apart. Lee and Neil ended up having a huge fight where they didn't speak for months. To be honest, I knew things were bad when John left – *because* he *had* left, and I knew that that might be the end of the band anyway but I still joined because… who wouldn't? A band like that? The chance was just too good to turn down."

According to Joyce, there was still a musical agenda.

"The plan had been to deck out the rehearsal rooms with recording gear like a studio and do the album there, because Lee was adamant that the sound would be right if we did it there, with the right gear."

It seems that Mavers was initially intent on recording all the early songs already on the album *again* for some sort of release (Go! Discs' La's album having been available and in the shops for well over a year by this point) and it was those songs which he still focused on.

"It was the same few songs again and again – the repetition which I mentioned before. He was working on the newer songs all the time, but he wouldn't let the band do them. We'd say, 'Come on, let's do something different, some new stuff, let's have the new songs' and Lee would say no. He'd look at you and say, '*You* lot aren't ready, you're *not ready* for the new songs.' And it would be back to 'Son of a Gun' or whatever. And we'd be trying to record bits and pieces at the same time – I think Lee was experimenting and trying to get the sound that he wanted.

"The thing was, though," Joyce smiles, "The new songs were so great, you *wanted* to stay in the band, you *wanted* to get to them. They really were – *are* – that good. And so, for a while, Lee's strict approach worked, if only because his songs were so brilliant.

"There's talk of a double album next time," says Joyce enticingly. "The new stuff *and* all the stuff that was fucked up before by the record company, but done properly…"

Mavers was reaching back to all the snippets of La's recordings – whether demos or live tapes – which he felt had the certain something he was looking for. Joyce mentions the tape recording of the Picket gig and confirms that it's actually himself and Neil Mavers and a few other friends who can be heard chattering on the tape in between songs.

"He took that tape, I recall, and with some bits was trying to record along with it, using it as the basis for what he wanted to do. Other bits of recordings, too. It was like everything was a tiny bit of a jigsaw puzzle that most of the time only Lee could see. Lee, you know, he's talented, very talented, so you know that, whatever he's doing, he's not wasting his time. It will be worth it. It's just that the tension was very bad and everything got more and more mixed up…"

Joyce's tone turns from simply regretful to more serious:

"Drugs were a big problem, by then. I was only just twenty when I joined the band. Being young and foolish, I didn't realise what was right in front of me, that they were all into it…"

Eventually, says Joyce, the time came when he realised what was going on within the band and he had to make his choice about what he was going to do.

"It was either get off or stay and…" his voice trails off.

He pauses for thought.

"Being in the band was all I wanted, I loved the music so much.

"So I stayed."

He turns away and looks out of one of the flat's windows for what seems like a long time.

It's not a pretty picture. After joining the band, gigging, and spending months rehearsing and attempting to record, things had deteriorated to the point where, by Joyce's own frank admission, "It got to the stage where it was just the drugs and then whatever else you could manage to fit round that, which wasn't much…

"Lee had this tape of music at this time and it was just – I think – four bars of music, four chords being played and looped and repeated over and over for the whole side of a cassette. Lee would just listen and listen to that for… days. It drove you mad."

There was only very occasional contact from Go! Discs. Joyce feels that the hostility was such that, on several occasions, it seemed that various band members and associates were actively trying to create problems with the label.

"I remember a couple of times that A&R men would come up from London to meet with us – you could tell that they were sort of trying to feel out the ground, find out what we were doing, you know: musically and generally. But… it was obvious that these suit guys were really shocked and were going to run back to London, telling tales of God knows what. And it probably wouldn't be as bad as the *actual truth*. After a couple of times like that, we didn't hear much else from them and what little money there was coming through stopped."

It's ironic that Joyce's decision to stay with the band (and in doing so become an addict himself) led to him finding himself more closely involved than ever with Mavers and his music. With Neil Mavers and Cammy drifting away (Cammy to a very brief stint in Power's embryonic Cast), Joyce was the only band member in regular musical contact with the chief La.

"Cammy and Neil got off and there was a period of time, probably a year or maybe eighteen months, where I'd be round at Lee's house and we'd sit together playing guitars amongst all that was going on at that time. It was through doing that I got to know most of the newer songs – new at that time. Of course, the drugs were still a big part of things…"

There was still optimism, though, Joyce makes clear.

"I stuck around for quite a while. There was always the possibility of doing something – little offers of work or gigs or whatever would always drift around, but Lee didn't really want to know."

One of these opportunities was the offer of a support slot for the reformed Madness at their Finsbury Park comeback gig in August of 1994. Mavers turned it down flat. Joyce was incensed:

"We were all skint and could have done with the money, but Lee was scraping by on his royalty cheques so… I think he was too embarrassed to play in front of all the music press that would be there, maybe because it would be the same old songs, no new ones… he knew the music wasn't together.

"But it was still a crazy time. I remember Lee had this Martin acoustic guitar[57] – really expensive – which someone had 'acquired' for him [*knowing nod from Joyce*]. I remember we did some searching around and found out that it was a very limited edition called 'The Tree of Life' and it had all this beautiful 'tree's branches' pattern inlay set into the fretboard. And Lee was well into that – the idea of it. I remember he was making plans to have his bathroom toilet seat made with the same design. And there was some guy or firm that were going to do it, too – god knows what it would have cost! I honestly don't know whether he did have it done in the end… this is what it was all like."

He shakes his head and laughs.

"Mad, fucked-up times…

"The new songs, though," he muses, "The new songs are great, fresher and more vibrant. There's no better songwriter than Lee as far as I'm concerned, and these newer songs – the ones I heard – they're obviously a progression for him as a writer: they're just *better* songs. If he never gets them out… well then, that'll be a shame, a real shame."

Joyce says that eventually pressures got too much and he and Mavers parted company. After struggling with his drug addiction, he managed to kick the habit and get back to focusing on music. His experience with hard drugs has left him with an interesting take on one lesser considered aspect of The La's:

"Looking at my own experience of drugs, which really came from being in the band – I look back now and I think The La's were a bit reckless and naïve about drugs and also *their* [the band's] influence on other people. Have you seen that 'The La's say skin up yer bastards!' thing?[58] Well, it certainly seemed to me that it was very easy to go from skinning up [i.e. having a joint] to harder things – there was a progression, born out of probably curiosity and peer pressure. And that's not a part of The La's which I think anyone should be proud of. Bands do have an influence on their fans. I look back on that, and I don't think it was a good thing."

But Joyce is also keen to stress his positive experiences from The La's.

"I do feel that I learned a lot from Lee, from that time when I was in the band. I learnt a lot about my instrument, the bass, and I learned about it as *an instrument* which is to say I think I've got a better idea what a musician's job is in a band. It's not about playing the loudest or the fastest or the best, not at all. When I joined The La's, I was playing with a pick [plectrum] and with everything turned up like most young players. But then, when I started playing with Lee, it was like: 'Hang on, I don't *need* it all turned up, I don't *need* a plectrum 'cause I can play all this stuff with just fingers and it still sounds solid and I can get the feel. The feeling is simple, so let's keep it that way.' That was such a realisation for me as a musician. And I've carried that ever since."

Joyce confirms the mythology which surrounds The La's for a lot of Liverpool musicians:

"Even though as a proper band when I was there we weren't together for that long, and then it was just Lee and me for a while, people sort of treat you a bit different: 'You played with Lee? No shit?' They want to work with you because of that. It's odd [*laughs*]…

"And it is true that a lot of legend surrounds them. I think a large part of that was the music, and then Lee not doing anything else musically. If you ask anyone around my age in Liverpool about The La's, most people will have an opinion, will remember something about them."

There was never any formal announcement that the band was at an end – indeed, Mavers continued to follow his muse as best he could. But the Cammy/Power/Neil Mavers line-up evaporated. Nobody who actually knew the band and those in it expected anything in the near future, if at all. To the world outside, though, the parting impression had been that The La's were going away to dream up a very different Album Number Two after being so unhappy with the first. Power had talked optimistically about this when interviewed on Radio One in 1991 prior to the group's live concert broadcast, so it seemed a sensible assumption.

But following his departure and the last few gigs after that, weeks of silence turned into months and months started to turn into a year and then beyond. Still there was no sign of Mavers or the next album. There would be the occasional 'Where are they now?' feature in the music press for the first couple of years but, very quickly, Mavers became a semi-mythic figure, a Mersey version of Fred Neil, a musical Howard Hughes for the music press to poke fun at.

'There She Goes' had become a radio perennial so he remained on the fringes of popular consciousness, occasionally bubbling to the surface when the song was used in a film soundtrack[59] or when another group covered it. The music weeklies would periodically report 'sightings' of Mavers or give uncorroborated accounts of his musical activities: Mavers seen in studio somewhere; Mavers apparently rehearsing with persons unknown somewhere in Liverpool; Mavers seen in audience at local gig; Mavers seen buying loaf of bread at corner shop...

The irony is that, by doing *nothing* (or appearing to), Mavers' reputation as gifted songsmith and truculent-but-visionary musician grew much faster and more intensely than if he'd simply buckled down to the second album straightaway. The magic of 'There She Goes' continued to enthral aspiring and successful musicians alike. They and a few die-hard fans kept the memory of what-might-have-been alive. The seed of the Lee Mavers enigma had been sown.

This, coupled with the absence of any definite announcement about the group's future, helped turn the Legend of The La's into something approaching a cult.

The Chinese whispers grew, suggesting, among other things, that Mavers had recorded two or three albums' worth of new material but wouldn't let anybody (especially the record company) hear or release it. Other stories suggested that, in a gigantic strop with Go! Discs, Mavers had vowed not to record anything at all ever again – or that he'd recorded all his songs on a tiny dictaphone recorder and was delighted with the result but Go! Discs wouldn't accept the sound quality. More depressing tales held that Mavers was existing in a constant drug-induced stupor in Huyton and would play his new songs for anyone who went round to his house with 'a little something'.

Whatever the truth, the stories convinced the casual reader that all was not well in La's land. Just when it seemed that the stories couldn't get any weirder, they *did*.

Against all the odds, it seemed, The La's were coming back.

Out of the blue, the band appeared on stage in February 1995 as support for Paul Weller (at that time a Go! Discs labelmate) in London. A line-up which consisted of Mavers in his usual guitar/vocals role, Neil Mavers on drums, new (and very young) recruit Lee Garnet on guitar and, inexplicably, Cammy now on bass. These last two choices seemed very odd in light of the enthusiastic but clearly limited playing ability of Lee Garnet. In contrast to all that had gone before and the established pattern of La's gigs (the rigid set list, in particular), an 'anything goes' rationale was in place.

The band covered songs by the Who, Bo Diddley and the Stones, mixed with a few La's originals, old and unheard. Even die-hard fans/commentators, trying to put a brave face on things, conceded that the word 'chaos' best described the night.

In what was probably the nadir of The La's' story, it appears that Mavers and the band – having played for a short period in which songs quickly descended into long drawn-out jams, sorely trying the patience of the audience – were unplugged by (allegedly) Weller's tour manager.

Following this, the 'band' made several appearances at various venues across the country, usually adopting 'hit-and-run' tactics whereby they were billed as 'Support' for other bands, and audiences turning up were surprised to find The La's as the opening act.[60]

The same unbridled enthusiasm/madness seemed to occur at each gig. One venue played was at the Hull Adelphi, long a stronghold for the band. Several years later, the promoter recalled the gig: "It was all madness, and very sad – for me. I think Lee played 'There She Goes' three times without realising it."

It was during this time that Joyce had his final contact with Mavers:

"I remember I was just walking down the street one day and out of the blue this van pulled up beside me with Lee in and Cammy and everyone and they were like: 'We're doing a gig tonight, are you coming with us?' Lee and I had already drifted apart and so I said no and that was that.

"I haven't seen Lee since then, which does make me sad. But it was important for me to get away from that situation and get clean and sort my life out."

Not too long after this the last proper interview with Mavers and The La's appeared in the music press. Never the most talkative of interviewees, Mavers had apparently sought out an NME journalist who was duly invited to the Liverpool rehearsal rooms, where the chief La held forth in what was certainly the longest and most detailed interview he's ever given.

Under the heading 'There He's Gone' (maybe a joke in itself given the tone of the interview), Mavers' interview by and large made for depressing reading. There was a clear gap between what the interviewer expected and what Mavers did (other band members – whoever they were[61] – although clearly present during the interview, say nothing) and he comes across as obscure in some places and downright odd in others, in between the occasional moment of clarity. Asked the inevitable question, he turns sharply on the interviewer:

"How long will it take for The La's to release a new album? As long as it takes, because that's how long it takes…"

On disagreeing with the interviewer about the sound of the new songs he has played for him:

"Nah, I think it sounds like a Nazi tank in Egypt somewhere, a panzer division TCH, TCH, BOOM!!"

The saddest part comes when the talk turns to recording:

"We got just the sound we wanted right here in the rehearsal room with just a little dictaphone, it was brilliant – not distorted or anything… [presumably turning to his bandmates] But we lost the tape somewhere, didn't we? In Hull, or somewhere…"

The accompanying portrait photo gives us the first (and last) proper look at the Lee Mavers of the mid-Nineties. Looking up to the camera positioned above him, there's a weariness in his face – no smile. His eyes have dark rings beneath them.

There are still moments of the old passion, though ("Songs… people hear the records and learn from them… it's a perfect thing, it's spirit and matter… One soul, one Nation!") but the interviewer sums things up well by concluding: "If only he could unlock the sounds in his head. These poor beautiful tortured La's…"

Time passed. Nothing more was heard until about two years later when Mavers gave another (very) brief interview to the NME, revealing that he had been "recording in a studio in London, the first new recording in five years." This all thanks to Go! Discs, with whom Mavers had seemingly mended fences ("Things were bad for a while but we had to go through that to get to here. None of this would have been possible without them"). The piece makes it clear that most of the new songs "are just jams really, with Mavers playing most of the instruments."[62]

There was a brief flicker of excitement when it was learned that he was playing with another Liverpool muso stalwart, bass player Edgar Summertyme, and that recording was continuing.

But as quickly as the flame of optimism for a La's renaissance was lit, it went out again. The recordings stopped and Mavers returned to Huyton.

Interviewed briefly about that time in one of the music weeklies, Summertyme had reported that: "We'd got a dead good sound – raw and earthy, but it wasn't anything that most labels would want to consider releasing commercially."

Former punk Rat Scabies, who owned the studio where the recordings/jams went on was quoted as saying that Mavers was on "fine form", the music "was flowing and great things would happen." They didn't. He packed up his guitar and went back to Liverpool.

And that was the last time the world heard from Lee Mavers.

Since then very little of substance has trickled through to the outside world – no more interviews, music or gigs. Even the rumours began to dry up. At least, it seemed that the same stories were being re-cycled with variations: Yes, there were lots of new Mavers songs. No, we wouldn't be hearing them any time soon. No, nobody's seen him for a while. Chinese La's whispers.

By this time, of course, the world had moved on. The explosion of new bands which had occurred under the banner of 'Britpop' reached its peak in 1995 and 1996 while Mavers was in exile (apart from that brief 'tour'). Oasis, the most significant of the new wave of bands to emerge, were led by Noel Gallagher, who declared early in his career that the job of Oasis, as he saw it, was "to finish what The La's had started."

Suddenly, it seemed, the whole country was full of bands who were alive to the spirit Mavers had been trying to drum up almost a decade earlier. The renaissance of the British guitarist and pop songwriter was in bloom and the man whose band had led the call was nowhere to be seen.

One of the acts at the forefront of 'Britpop' was Cast, John Power's band, whose conspicuous rise continued to cast a small glow on his 'old band' as people periodically asked: whatever happened to The La's anyway?

Joyce served time with The La's when the light of their magic was waning, and eventually went out. But he seems to have survived intact. He's upbeat and positive and – seemingly like all those who work with Mavers – very focused on his music and dedication to it.

Good for him.

Chapter X

"(Of sound) echoing, resounding, continuing to sound, reinforced or prolonged by vibration or reflection, responding to vibrations of a particular frequency, especially by itself strongly vibrating" – Definition of 'Resonance' from the Concise Oxford Dictionary

"My music is best understood by children" – Igor Stravinsky

Things finally grind to a halt.

I don't feel that I'm any closer to understanding the music of The La's or Mavers, despite all the research and interviewing I've done. In fact, it almost feels like I know less now than when I started – it seems the deeper you delve into this band's history, the harder it gets to sort out exactly what they were trying to say (let alone what actually went on!). And the harder it becomes to define their music.

There's no doubt that The La's commercial failure, if you want to put it that way, is part of the attraction, part of the enigma. The idea of great potential unfulfilled is almost more alluring than success. "There's no success like failure," Bob Dylan sang, "and failure's no success at all." We can love life's failures as much as its successful counterparts. The idea of the 'could've been, should've been' band or artist is one that music commentators (and fans) find appealing.

The La's are not the first to find themselves in this forlorn category. They're in very good company. Artists like Nick Drake, Big Star and Fred Neil[63] are all long-established residents of Palookaville. The allure of what could have been (and in The La's' case might still be) is very strong.

To add to my increasing dislocation, I'm starting to get resistance from potential sources – people I thought would be willing don't want to talk to me. Or people will only talk if Mavers has talked to me first and OK'd everything. I've encountered an invisible wall that I can't seem to penetrate, a wall of unreturned phone calls and unanswered letters. Only now do I realise that the run of luck I had with Badger/Hemmings/The Picket was exactly that, a run of very good luck.

I've exhausted all the leads I've uncovered so far. Except one. Someone who didn't really want to talk but who, after mild pestering, agreed as long as he remained anonymous. I agree to meet him since he sounds like he has something to say. He tells me he's a long time friend of Mavers although lately they've been out of touch. We meet up for an informal 'chat' (i.e. I only bring pad and pen, no tape recorder) in one of the Liverpool city-centre pubs.

I sit quietly in a corner with Mr X (as I'll refer to him) who has arrived before me and who, by his own admission, has already had a couple of beers. He tells me he has respect for what I'm trying to do. I confess that I've lately hit a bit of a brick wall and I can't seem to get a handle on what should be (in my opinion) a simple story.

"People don't understand. Musicians, especially, don't understand."

Mr X is holding forth as to how he perceives Mavers and his music.

"The key thing is that Lee wants the whole sound, that's the thing that matters most to him. Individuality isn't what it's about. You can sit at home and play your guitar if you want to be a musical individual but, if you want to be in a band, to play as a group, then you have to believe in that, because the four parts will add up to more than each individual. People working together – in anything – can create something transcendent and that's especially true with music."

It turns out that Mr X spent time with Mavers after The La's disappeared/disbanded. He has heard the new songs ("Totally mind-blowing"). In fact, he says that he was so enraptured by Mavers' music that it began to have an adverse affect on him.

"The songs... I had a little tape of them, the newer stuff, and I used to play it all the time. Eventually they just stayed in my brain and I couldn't get them out. I had various other problems and it all came to a head and seemed to crystallise within the music. So, for a while, I went off the rails a bit. I don't know what it was about the music that slipped into my subconscious.

"With Lee, the thing is, he keeps a child's mind for the music: he tries to hang onto that openness your mind has when you're little, because it's that simplistic approach that lets you tap into the music fully. Think about nursery songs: I bet you could sing me at least half a dozen now. Ask yourself why is that, since it's at least twenty years since you sang them? I don't have all the answers but it's obvious that they have a lasting and meaningful effect on you. That's what he strives for.

"And it's only that, so everything else just isn't important – fame or money or status or whatever – because, when you stack it up against the music, the real music, it's nothing."

But Mr X is quick to debunk any Mavers-as-god image.

"He doesn't invent anything new. There's no magic in that sense. He's just constantly trying to tap into that childlike way of thinking. When that happens, as he's the first to say, it just flows out. Everything's already out there for the taking. There's a line in one of his newer songs: 'You don't have to tell me because I've heard it all before.' That's the way it is. An ongoing cycle and you pull out of the ether what you want, but always remember it was there in the first place and you didn't invent it. You found it – which is Lee's gift, and a talent in itself – but you didn't create it.

"But people, especially musicians, hold him in such awe. You know? 'It's Lee!' And that gets in the way because, of course, the one thing he wants most of all is to find other musicians who can think the way he does, feel through the music the way he does. It's all so simple, that's the irony.

"The ultimate high for Lee is to play with a group of like-minded musicians and really tap into that source. The thing other musicians don't often realise is that, when that happens, the whole group become composers, regardless of who 'wrote' the song in some sort of legal sense or whatever. Each person is the songwriter when that happens, that's the key."

Here at last, perhaps, is the beginning of some sort of coherent reasoning behind the mystery, the uncovering of a kind of rationale, an explanation for the ever-changing line-ups, the endless re-recording.

What's more, when listening to some of the live recordings by the band, particularly the Picket tape, you start to hear the flow of the music. One thing suddenly becomes very clear: The La's album as released definitely does not flow in that same way. Mr X confirms this as not only his view but Mavers' as well. The talk turns to music the world over.

"Take the tribes in Africa or the villages in Morocco or wherever people are gathered and exist together in groups in a primitive way: music is a central part of their lives, a central part of their sociological existence. All the children know all the songs of the tribe and that is one of the best definitions of culture I can think of. Lee's brain works in the same way as that."

It seems the whole story of The La's and Mavers and his music begs the question: how far will you really go to get the thing that you want, how hard will you strive, how many times will you start again if you're not being true to yourself? Will you, in the words of Barry Sutton be "bought and sold" or will you aim for something higher and better, something that will *better you*, give you a clearer voice, a greater quality of expression? The La's strike deep into the heart of this dilemma with their music and their story.

Seen in this light, Mavers' continued attempts to re-record seem almost heroic. How many others would have started from scratch time and again? How tempting it must have been to accept the tapes from one of the many, many recording sessions and let it be released, for the sake of an easy life. Recalling again what Sutton had said: "Lee loved that music, you could tell, and so it was killing him that it wasn't happening like he wanted…"

How far are you prepared to go? Mavers, it seemed, was prepared to go to any lengths, any at all – even if that meant alienating his record company and his fans. His band too, if necessary.

For someone like Mavers, imbued with a strong sense of artistry and purpose, so immersed in his own music, compromise was out of the question. He clung to ideals he saw epitomised in his favourite artists – Beefheart, Bo Diddley, Chuck Berry – and held them up as his examples, seemingly missing or ignoring the fact that even those individuals would have had to compromise sometimes, if only because of the primitive recording techniques available to them.

He had unknowingly set himself on a collision course with his label and the music industry as a whole. In his defence, it was done from the purest of motives, the highest ideals, but with a large amount of naivety – for which it would be unfair to criticise him too much retrospectively. Aiming so high, you're almost bound to be disappointed, aren't you?

The only trouble with reaching so high is that, if things go wrong, there's a long way to fall. Which is just what The La's did, in the end.

Mr X checks his watch and tells me he's stayed a lot longer than he planned so I thank him and he's gone. I sit for a long while, thinking about what he's said, about how I feel about this journey that I'm on, and how I know now that it is a *journey*.

What started out as a simple idea is turning into an all-consuming quest, raising questions and issues which, for me anyway, are central to knowing what I am striving for, what I'm doing with my own life.

By what set of values am I prepared to write this book? Should that not extend to the rest of my life as well? Mavers once commented in an interview that he saw The La's as almost a representation and manifestation of life and its struggles. "The La's is a personal trip for the world," he said.

In his excellent book *High Fidelity*, Nick Hornby's central character, Rob, muses that "what makes songs so great is that they can take you forward while at the same time take you back to somewhere or something you felt." There's an incisive truth in that statement. Music is emotional: it can be a very intense experience, which is why most people have some sort of opinion about it. The emotional high combined with the feeling of community which a great song gives can, in the right hands, have a dynamite positive potential.

When you look at the bigger picture, what is more important than communication, touching another person's heart and providing that emotional high, that emotional connection? For an artist, in the true definition of that word, not a lot.

At their best, songs are emotional touchstones, postcards sent out by an individual to the larger world, the signposts of our life's journey. I will wager with all readers now that they can't name half the English monarchs of the last three hundred years but I'm sure each one can at least hum the tune of 'Scarborough Fair' or 'Greensleeves' or sing a few bars of Beethoven. Shouldn't we as individuals be striving for something that can be on this level, whether it's within the field of music or sport or writing or any arena?

Perhaps it seems like music (the song) is being elevated to some sort of undeserved higher level of importance here. Maybe. But how else do you explain its continued importance in so many people's lives (my own included) and society generally? The Hare Krishna movement is dedicated to finding spiritual enlightenment for individuals purely through music (chanting simple phrases) and dance, and very little else.

Music, *the right music*, has power. The right music can change lives, change minds, influence feelings and emotion. That, in a world which is increasingly focused on wealth and commercial success and material acquisition, is real power. But it's a power with vintage roots, an old power, a power that has perhaps as much subconscious effect as conscious, and that sets it aside from most other things. Born when man first started to bash rocks or bones together in rhythm thousands of years ago, it has been with us ever since. Real power.

Resonance.

It's from the search for this type of music – the music – that the call(in' all) from The La's comes, they and the few others like them. The real tragedy of The La's' story is not found in the missed opportunities or the (seemingly) wasted talent of Lee Mavers, but in the realisation that so few people heard, and understood, what he was trying to say about the way he wanted people to hear his music. There can be little doubt that Mavers was aware of his reputation as an eccentric: he may well have played up to people's notion of this when it suited. Fundamentally, however, he wanted to serve his muse.

It is the central irony of the story of The La's that something so simple appears so complicated.

I make the decision. I'm going to take this as far as I can. If that means the book takes years to write, then so be it. I'm going to try to follow the example The La's set and I'm not going to paste over cracks and difficult issues, I'm going to try to get to heart of it all, to the end of this story, to this journey's end.

I can't leave it alone now. I need to see the film through to the final reel. I need to know if all I've done so far and all that's left will be worth it, will be justified, will be what I secretly hope for. It's time to see if the water is deep or not, and there's only one way to do that – I have to jump in.

Chapter Eleven
Raindance
(Or, Adventures close up to the Lightbulb)

"The plain fact is that music per se means nothing: it is sheer sound, and the interpreter can do no more with it than his own capacities, mental and spiritual, will allow. And the same applies to the listener"
– Sir Thomas Beecham

It's a cold Friday in November as I speed through the Liverpool back streets in my small car. I have to wipe my windscreen periodically to stop it misting up, as countless shop fronts, cars and people's faces speed past outside.

Lee Anthony Mavers, in the passenger seat, is talking incessantly. Skipping quickly from one topic of conversation to another: unemployment, the city of Liverpool and the breakdown of community in society, Thatcherism, Everton football club and guitar repairers. Jasper, in the back, banters backward and forward with Mavers – they're old friends and it seems as though everything they talk about forms part of a long discussion they've been having forever. I'm trying to listen (and join in now and again) but I need to keep my eye on the road.

Mavers periodically directs me to go left or right, down ever-smaller backstreets. It's amazing to me how he knows his way – we're on the other side of the city from where he lives and we must have travelled five or six miles and taken at least two dozen sharp turns in quick succession before he finally tells me to pull up in a dead-end street apparently no different from hundreds we've passed. We get out and Mavers disappears over the road into the yard of one of the houses nearby. We follow. When we get into the small yard, he's fumbling with a chunky padlock which secures a big green door: that's when it hits me.

I turn back, go outside and look up at the house: I realise that I've been here before, been to this house before – the very same house.

But how have I got here? Well, let's take a step back in time.

After I decide that I want to talk to Mavers – or, at least, to see if he wants to talk – I toy with ideas of how to get to speak to him. I don't know where he lives exactly, but various sources offer to either take me or make an introduction, but I don't get the impression that any of them are regularly in touch with him, and I don't want to make a bad first impression. I also rule out finding where he lives and just turning up unannounced – I wouldn't be best pleased if someone turned up on my door step, and I want to avoid coming across like some nutty neo-Mark Chapman.

In the end, as with so much that has happened to me while I've been doing this, it's simple luck. I go to interview a source who, unbeknown to me, rings Mavers just after I've left him. He comes out to find me and catches me up. Before I know it, I'm being driven to Huyton for an audience with the man himself, who is apparently keen to meet me (at least, he didn't say he didn't want to meet me).

Not expecting to meet Mavers at such short notice, I'm not at all prepared with any detailed questions or anything, so I put all my hope in coming across as sincere and focused in what I'm trying to do. It's not easy, though. I've never actually met anybody 'famous' before and, whichever way you look at it, he is famous, to a degree. Plus, he is someone I am increasingly starting to admire as a musician and songwriter and, dammit, artist.

I can't help but have butterflies in my stomach.

I don't know it at the time but, as we travel to Mavers' house, I'm about to start realising how wrong some of the sources I've talked to have been, and how wrong I've been about some of the assumptions I've made. I get the first sense of this when we pull into the driveway of Mavers' house. I can't honestly say what I was expecting, but it wasn't anything as, well, normal as what I actually find. It's just a semi-detached house on a street. Maybe part of me was expecting big neon signs: "La's Central" or "The bloke who wrote 'There She Goes' lives here!" I don't know. I decide that this is my first taste of the difference between rock'n'roll reality and real-world reality.

We pull up and get out of the car. My heart is racing. I toy with the idea of doing a runner there and then. Two thoughts run through my mind. The first is a comment someone once made about Marianne Faithfull: "She's the caretaker of her own legend." I remember thinking about that for a long time and eventually deciding that it was more criticism than compliment. Ever since it's bothered me that maybe I'll find the same true of Mavers. The other thing I keep recalling is the old adage that you should never meet your heroes because you'll always come away disappointed. How can any person ever really live up to your expectations of them? We never stop to recognise how unrealistic admiration and adoration can be. I don't want to be disappointed by Mavers. Anyone else: fine. But I badly don't want to be disappointed after meeting him.

My source knocks on the door and, after a pause, it opens. Standing there, although older, leaner, with much shorter hair and a baby under his arm, is unmistakably Lee Mavers.

"Alright, la, how's it going?"

"Fine. You?" I reply

"Yeah, sound, la, sound."

It turns out that this is all I manage to say for about an hour – I'm grateful that my source and Mavers haven't seen each other for a while because they chat away, catching up on this and that. We go into the lounge and I'm introduced to Jasper, who's also there, but I sit saying almost nothing while the three of them talk, just sort of nodding at various times so I don't seem impolite.

Inside Mavers' house things are, again, not what I expect. There are no La's posters on the walls advertising old gigs or the like. No massive collection of vinyl (in my mind, it could only be vinyl). Worryingly, there don't seem to be any guitars, either. In fact, the only thing obvious from a quick inspection is that children live there – toys and colouring books sit stacked in corners or on sides. Children's shouts can be heard somewhere deeper in the house, but it's quiet in the lounge. The television is on, tuned to the football results with the sound turned down.

I decide that whipping out my tape recorder and stuffing it under Mavers' nose isn't a great idea. It just doesn't seem right. He turns to me finally.

"So, why are you wanting to write a book about The La's?"

They all turn to look at me, and I'm struck dumb for a moment. Then I launch into a brief summary of what I've written in the introduction to this book, tagging on a bit about how much I admire the music and how much I admire Mavers' songwriting, and how chuffed I am to actually be able to meet him. He cuts me short with "I'm only a man, la, just a person" but he says it indulgently so I don't feel too bad.

Then I say that I feel I have to ask on behalf of all La's fans: will any more music come out?

"It's been hard, la. I can feel it coming back again, pulling me back [the music] and I have to go with that when I feel it."

This seems to break the ice a little more and we start talking about The

La's' album. He tells me it's shit, that I should really hear the early demos. Before I know it, he's produced an old tape and slotted in into his hi-fi and the sound of 'Son of a Gun' is flooding the lounge. It's cleaner, sharper and more together than the album version. The music draws Mavers' children into the room – young boy and girl, both about ten or eleven, and baby twins who, you can tell, have only just started walking.

An electric guitar-powered 'Liberty Ship' comes on next and suddenly Mavers' eldest son is jumping onto the windowsill and chanting out the verses which he obviously knows by heart:

> I am the sailor, the ocean slave
> Fill your sail with the breath I gave...

Things start to get a little surreal when Mavers tells him to calm down and come down. The two of them end up chasing round the sofa I'm sat on while the music plays.

Eventually, things (and children) do calm down and my source and Jasper head home, leaving Mavers and I alone. It's getting dark outside now and I make my pitch to him about this 'journey' that I'm on and wanting to talk about the band and their story. He tells me he'd be pleased to help and spend time talking. Before I know it, he is talking, reminiscing about the time he wrote 'There She Goes'.

"I remember one night I was just running up and down the G scale on those top two strings and whoa! There it was, that riff, and then everything else just fell into place and it just swept me away."

Inspired, he rushes from the room and comes back with a guitar. He enthuses to me about the new tuning or way of tuning that he's come across, and how it makes the songs ring out. To demonstrate, he gives me a quick burst of the Stones' 'Jumping Jack Flash'. It's great. Part of me is already kicking myself for not taping all this, but it still doesn't feel right, and I'm determined to go with my instinct. I ask about fixing up a time to meet. It's clear that weekends are far too loud and hectic with his children being around, so we try to pick a weekday in the near future. He reaches behind him for his diary and starts checking dates. I look closer. It's not a diary: it's this season's Everton fixtures list. I smile.

We talk a bit more and he lends me the demo tape he's been playing and a very tatty-looking book about the Beatles which he tells me really inspired him when he read it. Eventually I have to leave to catch my train. On the way home, I'm filled with a sense of having achieved what I initially set out to do – I've met Mavers, shaken his hand, told him I think his songs are great. I know I'm still going to carry on with the larger task of the book but, for now,

I've got this top-of-the-mountain-after-a-big-climb feeling.

Over the coming days, we speak a few times on the phone. He tells me he's recently started renting a little place which he's kitted out to record. Do I think it would be a good idea to go there and listen to some of the new songs? You bet I do.

That is how I come to be standing outside said house deep in the Liverpool suburbs, after having driven Mavers and the ever-present Jasper across the city.

I know for definite that I've been here before because this is the very house that I came to see Mike Badger at, only he was upstairs and we're going in downstairs (it's effectively two different properties, flat above and ground floor below). Mavers and Badger each renting different parts of the same house? Talk about coincidence. Except it isn't, but we'll come to that.

We go inside. It's dark. One large frosted window at the end has to light the whole room – and it's a long, deep room. It's also cold, really freezing, and I can see Mavers' breath in the air as he fiddles with a small gas heater which has seen better days. The lights go on and I see the room properly for the first time.

It's obvious now why Mavers' house was (almost) devoid of guitars, because they're all here: black-and-white Fender Stratocaster, red Fifties Telecaster, what looks like an original Sixties Hofner bass (the kind Paul McCartney used to play in the Beatles), various acoustics and a few other guitars I don't recognise. One of the equipment cases stacked to the side has stencilled lettering on it: P Townshend. There's also a drum kit set up, loads of amplifiers and, at the far end of the room, several mikes are positioned on stands ready for use. I hear Mavers flick on a switch somewhere and red power-on lights glow from several of the amps. I hear white noise arrive in the background. On a small makeshift table sits a large pad on which are written lots of tantalising new song titles, none of which I recognise: 'Human Race', 'Robberman', 'She Came Down' and 'Raindance'.

It's still freezing. While Jasper sets about brewing something warm from the kettle, Mavers leads me to the far end of the room where the most amazing recording desk I've ever seen sits. It's not much larger than an average office desk – making it smaller then most modern music recording desks – but any other comparisons end there. It looks as though it was made in the late Fifties or early Sixties – it has lots of military-style dials and big, chunky knobs – and looks to be in immaculate condition, absolutely immaculate. As though it was made yesterday and time-warped into the present.

Mavers looks at it with genuine affection and runs his hand over the dials and knobs. He ducks behind and starts flicking switches again. Lights on the desk glow with life. He starts telling me about how the desk's gold contact points mean that the maximum amount of signal can pass through, so the sound is as true as possible, how the volume can be pushed way up without distortion in the sound quality. In short, it's the desk to end all desks.

Jasper brings over three cups of steaming something and we slump down into the soft but cold sofa chairs.

Myths about Lee Mavers as propagated by the music media and others: he is moody and sullen, uncommunicative and, when he does find it in him to talk, it's in a sort of a scouse psychobabble where very other word is "la" and no-one really understands what he's on about.

The truth about Lee Mavers as witnessed by the author of this book: he is friendly and eager to talk, warm, passionate and intense about those things he cares about, and often very, very funny. Great company, in short.

That said, there is something quite different about him. This is clear when we talk: it's not that you can't understand what he's saying, but you do have to pay attention, because topics of conversation change quickly and lots of images are used to punctuate and expand on what he's trying to tell you. At times, little snippets of song lyrics and paraphrases creep into what he's saying. At one point, he says: "...that's because I owe you and you owe me and I see you can stand on your own two feet..."

It's clear, though, that today is a "bad" day for Mavers – he tells me this at the outset. Still, he's keen to play me some of the new stuff he's done. He seems tired and subdued throughout, so I decide just to soak up the atmosphere (such as it is) and take in as much as I can.

I tell Mavers that I've been to the same place before to meet up with Mike Badger. He doesn't seem too surprised. Then I notice that one of the guitars in the room is very similar to the guitar Badger had when I interviewed him. In fact, when I give it a closer inspection, I realise (for reasons too boring to interest to anyone other than guitar players) that this is the same guitar. I mention this to Mavers. Something obviously clicks within him: he starts telling me the story behind these apparent coincidences.

It turns out that the guitar is Mavers' rather then Badger's. So why did Badger have it then? Answer: because Mavers and Badger had recently been working together again for the first time in over a decade. This is something of a La's revelation so I ask all about it. It's clear straightaway though that things haven't gone well with the resurrected team of Mavers and Badger. Through a process of elimination, Mavers and I work out that, at the time I went to see Badger, Badger was in fact working with Mavers.

Yet Badger said nothing about it to me – indeed, gave the impression that he only saw the chief La "now and again." Why?

When I first went to see Mavers at his house, he pulled out a copy of a record entitled Break Loose – the early La's.[64] He told me that it had just come out, but little else was said. It turns out that this was released on Badger's 'Viper' label – indeed, the idea for the album itself was conceived by Badger, but without any input from Mavers. In fact, it seems that Mavers knew nothing about it. This is the problem.

"If he'd have come to me and said, 'Look, this is what I want to do,' I would have probably helped him, but it was all secretive and hushed."

Mavers and Badger had started playing together, but Mavers says he felt Badger's heart wasn't in it. Now he feels that Badger was only pretending to be interested in playing and writing in order to get Mavers to OK the release of this 'new' La's record. Some of the songs on Break Loose – including 'Sweet 35' and 'My Girl Sits...' – are obviously joint Mavers/Badger compositions, and Mavers is playing guitar on most of the other tracks. But Mavers had no say in the record, and has received no money from it. ("Time and again, I keep making the same mistake which is having too much trust in people, too much trust in human nature," he tells me). More than that, it's obvious that he feels betrayed by a friend and (so he thought) fellow-believer, and also by what he sees as substandard material out under The La's' banner ("A bunch of shite-sounding demos" is how he describes what he's heard of the record).

"Badger, he may not have had it musically, but he's one of the only people that I've met who've had the same sense of..." Mavers gestures to indicate a cross between inspiration and, I think, some sort of larger spirituality.

The experience has left him bitter and critical towards his old collaborator.

He can't explain why Badger didn't tell me they were collaborating again ("Probably because he knew it wouldn't come to anything") nor why Badger told me Mavers wouldn't want to talk to me.

We drop the subject. Mavers picks up the red 1950s Fender Telecaster which has been lying against the wall and starts to tune it. Eventually he plugs it into an amplifier and a warm, gently distorted guitar sound fills the room. For a moment, he picks out the introduction to 'There She Goes'. My heart skips a beat.

He's standing amongst the microphones. When I look closer, I see they are old-style radio-announcer type mikes, the kind that Neil at the Picket was telling me about.

He steps up to one of them.

> Where have you been my blue eyed son,
> Where have you been my darlin' young one?

He looks over to me. "Is that Dylan?"

I nod, and he drifts through a couple of verses of 'A Hard Rain's A-Gonna Fall' before stopping to tune again. He then begins again with another song, which I don't recognise but assume is a cover, and his voice starts to hit out clearer even as he's singing – it's the same voice that I've heard many times on record but never in person. It's a lovely song, and Mavers chants out the same line: "Never stop the rain, never stop the rain…" Quickly, though, it descends into more tuning. He explains that he's having problems with this, his favourite guitar. The intonation isn't quite right, which means he can't tune it perfectly.

Seemingly giving up on the electric guitar, he picks up an acoustic and starts fingering out some jazzy-style four-chord progression which he plays over and over:

> If you open your mind…
> If you open your mind…
> If you open your mind…

The same line again and again, like a mantra: it does feel quite hypnotic. His voice starts reaching for higher notes.

"Voice is coming back," he mutters.

Throwing down the acoustic, he leaps to the drums and starts hammering out the rhythm to the song, still perfectly in time with what he was playing on the guitar. Between putting down the acoustic to getting to the drums, the music stopped for Jasper and I but it was still going in Mavers' head. He just carried on with the next instrument he came to.

Eventually he comes back to where we're sitting. The conversation turns to music, modern music in particular.

"I feel like one of the last musicians or one of the last believers or whatever you want to call it – I mean who else is there really trying to capture the feeling? Who? Sometimes I sit and think about it and it seems that 'There She Goes' is the only song in the last ten-odd years."

This would be an extremely egotistical thing to say, if Mavers didn't have a look of total desperation when saying it.

"I don't know what's happened in the last decade, the Nineties, it's just as though everything's been the wrong way round."

So the Eighties were great, then, halcyon days?

"Well, the music wasn't all great, but there was just this feeling, this optimism or forward motion. Just a wave that you felt you were riding on, everyone was on, but in the Nineties... I don't know what happened.

"Sometimes, it's just a heavy weight, it's like no one else understands. It's all: 'Me! Mine! That's mine!' People don't want to play the real music anymore."

But doesn't he want to inspire and communicate with his audience, the whole audience? In what must be the darkest moment of this bleak afternoon, Mavers turns to me and holds out his hands.

"But the audience is corrupt – or they've been corrupted."

I tackle him on this.

"Not everyone, but most. It's like, the last ten years, even if you had something to say, nobody would have listened anyway, so what was the point?"

He looks over at the red Telecaster which he'd spent a good part of the afternoon trying to tune.

"To be honest, unless I can get that guitar fixed so I can tune it, I can't see me ever doing anything again..."

His words hang in the air and I'm filled with a sense of total frustration. I want to box Mavers' ears in an attempt to shake him out of this mood, remind him how great his songs are, that nothing so trivial as an awkward guitar should get in his way.

The talk turns to bands, and The La's specifically.

"People think that I'm some great dictator or something, but I'm not, not at all. All I want is to find people who believe the way I do, feel the way I do: 'All for one and one for all.' Instead, it's been 'all for one and none for all'. I don't want to be first fiddle, I'd rather be four fiddles in a row. It's like a ship at sea: everyone is vital, engine stoker and officer – you can't have one without the other. But all I know how to do is navigate. It's all I've ever known. I can see form – that's all it is. Music is all I've ever wanted."

That desperate look is back in his face again.

Mavers goes over to a locked metal cupboard and takes out a box containing reels of tape. He flips more switches near the desk and a sound which can only be described as "from the grave" fills the room.

"It takes a few minutes for the machine to warm up until it hits the right speed."

We all smile. It's like listening to music underwater – or maybe in the womb.

Eventually, the tape speeds up and what sounds like "proper" music kicks in. It's a full band – rough, but not at all unlistenable. It's bright, earthy, clearly La's: "She came down in the morning/She came down in the morning..."

Taking a look in the cupboard the tape came from, I can see lots of other boxes. So who's Mavers been recording with then?

"Oh, it's all me, la – one thing at a time: drums, then guitar or bass."

So, it appears that the only person Lee Mavers has so far felt able to record with, is Lee Mavers. That seems to sum up a lot of what this afternoon is about.

Heading back through the winding back streets, Mavers is talking again about what he sees as the problems of the last decade.

"It's – I know people will get at me for saying this but Thatcher was right: there isn't any society, only family groups and friends. But people have only just been realising that – and it's hard to come to terms with, in some ways. It's all been a fog. Lately, I've felt like I've been staring at this big light bulb constantly, and it's just... I've been too close up to it."

Back at Mavers' house, he puts the kettle on. Jasper having gone home, we sit around deciding what to have for tea (I haven't eaten since breakfast). Mavers pulls over a nearby guitar and starts strumming the same chords that I'd heard him play earlier in the day, and assumed to be a cover. Now I'm not so sure.

"What is that?"

"'Raindance': I played it today, thought you knew it from the way you were nodding along..."

And he proceeds to play me what must be most of the song, only to throw down the guitar and dash off when the boiling kettle whistles. I sit stunned. The song is brilliant, completely brilliant – all the songs I've heard today are good, but this one is touched with the same magic as 'There She Goes'. That is obvious even to (relatively ignorant) me. Not that the two songs have much in common or are musically that similar, but you can tell they both come from the same mould. It's the difference between a great song, and a classic one. Corny as that sounds, it's the only description which seems to fit.

In one moment, all the cobwebs and dark clouds of the day have been swept away, or at least put into a longer perspective. I'm reminded why I was moved to start all this in the first place.

Over fish and chips, I'm treated to a potted history of Everton football club. Mavers makes it clear that he sees a similarity between his own fortunes and those of his favourite team – success and generally getting it together in the nineteen-eighties and disillusionment and lack of focus in the Nineties.

It's dark by the time I get ready to leave. I shake Mavers' hand. I've done absolutely no taping at all during the whole day and asked none of the questions I'd wanted to, so we agree to meet again. I promise him that it will be a thorough sit down and talk-through of everything, and he's keen to do it. I give him a draft of the introduction to this book and the first couple of chapters and then I'm on my way.

I've been driving for about an hour when my little mobile phone starts to ring: it's Mavers, enthusing about the drafts I've let him see. He asks me not to change a word of the introduction, saying it's the best introduction he's read to a music book. He gets stuck for words momentarily.

"It's just… I'm so pleased that you get from the music what you do, that's the thing, the main thing, the only thing…"

He says he's ready to put me right on some things which Badger and Hemmings have said, and to correct my spelling! I feel that maybe I'm starting to make some headway with this job I've started.

"The feeling I get, la," he says just before we hang up, "Is that you're involved now. You might be thinking, 'Well, I just want to do the book,' but, take it from me, you're involved."

Chapter Twelve
The Oral History of The La's
(as told by Lee Mavers)
Part One

"I don't want to sell my music. I'd like to give it away because, where I got it, you didn't have to pay for it" – Captain Beefheart

"You can reach a point in the creation of something where the trappings and the tinsel and the construction become so important that it doesn't really matter at all what's inside. The show can be a total contrivance: ultra-formulaic music, jive bits of business for punctuation, cabooses loaded with props, choreographed postures and preenings, even the audience enlisted to give it right back on cue, educated in the process through past concerts and festival movies. The whole thing can be just that vacuous, and because someone has taken the trouble to entertain them, everybody still goes away happy. Showbiz is funny that way" – from 'Jethro Tull in Vietnam', Lester Bangs, *1973*

The new millennium arrives. A couple of weeks into January 2000, I'm back at Mavers' again. It's late on a Friday morning when we settle down in front of the fire in his living room. I'm supplying the tape (my bag is full of blank cassettes) and he's supplying the coffee and toast. We're digging in for the duration – I tell him I want to hear as much as he wants to say.

It's a different Mavers to the downcast soul I last met before Christmas just passed. He's extremely upbeat and filled with a sense of momentum, telling me that he really feels things 'moving back to where they should be' and he's ready to talk about the past. I take a deep breath and press the record button.

"I was into The Stranglers when I was younger – I loved those Jean Jaques Burnel mad bass lines and I really wanted to play like that. And I did, after learning to play the bass on an old guitar which only had a couple of the bass strings on it. When I'd be grounded, I'd be up in my room playing. I had some Stranglers songs, so I just learnt off the records. That was my early experience with music – the bass. Guitar came later.

"I eventually got a proper bass for my eighteenth birthday. My mate, who had a mate who played in a band, said that he'd found this old Fender bass and it was seventy quid. And so I managed to convince my dad to get it for me.

"The day I got it, I was out in town with a friend and we bumped into a mate of his who was in a band – and they needed a bass player! So I heard some of their stuff on a tape and I thought it was great. I was in that band for about a year-and-a-half."

This was Huyton's proto-punks, Neuklon.

"I did a few gigs with them, just hanging around playing the bass really. Learning to play the bass and biding my time. And that was it. That was Neuklon."

And Neuklon was the start of the road that would lead Mavers to Mike Badger.

"The first time I met Mike Badger was on a Saturday afternoon, I think. I went to a mate's house and Badger turned up in a yellow biker's jacket with a big cravat and all mad stuff on, because he was like 'arty'.

"After then, we saw each other maybe four times over the next couple of years. Hardly at all, really. The next real time that I recall was when we met in the Bistro around '84 – we first met around 1980 – so that's the length of time between."

Mavers relays the story behind him and Badger meeting up, and it tallies almost exactly with Badger's version of events:

"He'd just come back from London, where I'd been as well at the same time. And that Saturday, I think it was, I was in the Bistro and Badger was there and we had a little chat, talked about Beefheart – I'd been listening to *Trout Mask Replica* – and it just led on from there.

"So, a week or so later, we spoke on the phone and agreed we were up for doing something and he came round. We went up to the quiet top corner of the house and he just opened his bag and threw out all these sheets with his words on and I started looking through it. The first thing I saw was 'Red Deer Stalk' and I was: [mimes picking up the guitar] De de de, De de DE! It was dead easy, really. It just came out, and he was dead pleased: 'Yeah, that's great! That's great!'

"The words… well, they weren't that great but it was a start."

But Mavers has a different slant on their 'collaboration'.

"He was dead into it, wanted to keep getting together, and I was like: 'Well, you supply the weed and I'll keep coming round or whatever.' It was that kind of vibe.

"We did a bit of recording, at his instigation, and it was all his lyrics and my music. We recorded 'Red Deer Stalk', 'I Did The Painting', 'The Time Is Right' and 'Soho Wendy'."

Mavers suddenly adopts the most hilarious foppish art-house pretentious voice it's possible to imagine: "Soho Wendy, Soho Wendy/She's coming home on Tuesday or Wednesday…"

So he wasn't all that keen on some of Badger's lyrics, then?

"You can imagine us all playing behind him [Badger], laughing our heads off, bum notes the lot. He was just…"

Mavers pauses for what seems like an eternity, obviously searching for the right word to reflect his sense of disgust.

"…Morrissey."

This is clearly a different perspective than Badger had of that formative period.

Mavers: "I didn't take it seriously. I already had my own songs. By that time I'd written 'Clean Prophet', which was my first song."

He goes on.

"I already had my own dream or idea or whatever. I'd come back from London because I'd decided to get myself a guitar and make a start. And 'Clean Prophet' was it.

"When we recorded 'Sweet 35', I remember, we'd come to the end of the session and had some time over, so I just grabbed Badger's lyric sheets. The first thing I saw was 'Sweet Thirty-Five' and it matched with a little riff that I'd been playing the day before and Boom! There it was. So we had a run-through and then recorded it. And we *still* had some time after that, so we jammed 'Dovecot Dub', or what became that. We were just having a laugh, really. We didn't even have any amps. We just plugged straight into the wall![65]

"We were lucky that the engineer was good and he managed to get a fairly good sound from very very basic equipment. He effectively produced us."

Mavers is suddenly reflective. He looks past me, out of the lounge window. The fire is crackling quietly.

"Honest, honest to God, I never *ever* thought we'd have a problem with recording until later on when I saw that it was going wrong. But those early sessions? It was OK, not *great*, but then who was worrying then? Not me."

Mavers is suddenly overcome by a small wave of nostalgia:

"It was beautiful, that studio [the Attic], especially later, when I was doing my own stuff there."

This was in August '86 session, which saw Mavers making a serious effort to record his material for the first time. But he immediately hit a barrier.

"It was clear from Day One that I didn't have the language, the terminology of the studio. I was trying to capture a definite sound, but I didn't think I could say 'I want a *Beggar's Banquet*[66] acoustic sound' or something like that. I didn't know what the guy knew or didn't know about bands. So I would have got a better sound, if I'd known more.

"Anyway, they were only demos," says Mavers, tackling one of The La's' most enduring myths.

"People think that I say those demos are the gospel. They're not. They're just a photograph, and not a great one, but the album isn't even *near that*. I'd rather take them on a desert island than that album any day. The demos are warm and they've got vibe and character – that's all. It was when we put all the various rough demos together on one tape that I realised it wasn't so bad. They all had a consistent sound, a quality, a character.

"All I've ever been after is capturing all the rawness in a 'Hollywood' production: all the demos are is the rawness in a demo production."

The talk returns to his musical relationship with Mike Badger.

"And so we weren't hanging round all the time. It wasn't some big get-together, not at all. I'm not saying that to be nasty, I'm saying it because it's true.

"Pretty quickly, I had 'Clean Prophet' and 'Endless' and probably 'Come In, Come Out', too, by that time.

"So every now and then Badger and I get together and we play a bit. Well, he's actually not playing yet. He didn't start playing until about '86."

The way Mavers explains it, the first time he played live with The La's, it all came out of the blue.

"So I get a call from Badger in early '86 – we hadn't seen each other for quite a while then: 'We're doing a gig and we need a guitarist, will you help us out?'

"At the gig, I remember just riffing anything, anything at all – I'd only been playing over a year so I was still cutting my teeth. It was mad…

"And that was it, I wasn't 'in' the band or anything, I wasn't taking it seriously. Good lads, but not really going anywhere musically. But it was around these times that we pooled our resources to do that early recording I've mentioned.

"Then, another gig, and then another, because people kept dropping in and out of the group. Around this time, I found out that 'Reindeer' and 'Sweet 35' are on a record!"

Mavers apparently hadn't been told about his first-ever record release.

"Badger was like: 'Oh yeah, oh yeah.' And there's no mention of me, at all. Despite the fact that I wrote all the music, virtually."

Meanwhile, the occasional gigs continued ("I still wasn't part of the band at that point") and Mavers hatched a small plan for himself:

"I got it into my head to get a Volkswagen caravanette and fuck off to Europe with a guitar and these songs, and see what happened."

It turns out that this was largely due to his dissatisfaction with Liverpool, which debunks another La's myth: the worship of all things Mersey.

"I'd even thought about going to *Manchester* [*Mavers utters the name of the city with a tone of such disgust you'd think he'd rather molest children than go there*]… because here just seemed dead, somewhere I'd never escape from…

"But then, a friend of mine offered me a gig in mid-'86. Badger was around and we ended up doing half his stuff and half mine, and I suddenly realised that this was maybe something that I ought to think again about. Badger was so keen to do something that I got to thinking, 'Okay, let's do it then.'

"And then one gig was leading to another. I think it was just after that gig a friend told me that someone had heard about *another* gig, so we all piled in a taxi and off we went. And that was the Sefton gig, where I met Barry [Sutton] for the first time and saw Marshmallow Overcoat."[67]

Mavers, now committed to The La's and gigging regularly, felt the surge of momentum.

"It was – you just knew it – like Badger said about the wave creeping up on you. We were standing on a surfboard. Eventually, if you wait long enough, the wave comes and sweeps you up."

But the wave wasn't there just yet. Continued line-up changes didn't help. A succession of mediocre (at best) friends-of-friends musicians and others who just weren't interested continued to frustrate Mavers – and Badger, no doubt.

Then there was the matter of the band's name.

"I don't think I ever really knew what our name was until we had a small press review, and it was 'Stand High for The La's' or something. And I was like*: [turns to Badger's phantom while reading review]* 'The La's?! *The La's??!!!*'"

Back to mid-'86, however, and Mike Badger's newest friend at the time:

"Badger had gone on that course [the council-run musician's scheme] and met John Power. People kept coming and going in the band and I was always saying to Badger: 'We need people who are committed.' We were always hoping to find people who felt the way we did, who would stay on."

Mavers hadn't gone on the music scheme.

"I didn't even try to get on it. Go and learn music in school? I'm sorry, but you don't, la. You learn it yourself – there's no other way. School is no substitute for experience. There *is* no substitute for experience is there? You can't have a mathematical formula for soul."

But Badger *was* on the scheme, and that led to Mavers meeting Power.

"John came down about a week or two after Badger suggesting we try him out. It seemed that he was more like *me* than Badger, if you know what I mean. He was just a little seventeen-year-old whippersnapper, a kid, but he was whipping and snapping that bass guitar nice. Alright, it was raw and rough but, if I told him to play something, he'd do it.

"He was just blown away by the music, so there was the trio there, right there. It wasn't long after that that 'Callin' All' came about."

I ask about 'Callin' All', considered one of The La's best songs, allegedly a true Badger/Mavers collaboration. When I mention this, it's clear that Mavers doesn't see it that way at all.

"If you look at it in terms of who's done what: the lyrics were written by me over a year earlier. The guitar parts – well, that was *my* riff and *my* chords. My melody, as well. It's just that, when we jammed it, Badger just phrased a couple of guitar chords differently, played them slightly differently and that triggered me off. It was just: Boom! I went into a corner and changed the rhythm playing a bit, and that was the final piece of the jigsaw for me. I knew I had the whole song then.

"Now, on that basis, someone's going to get a writing credit? What fraction of a percentage does he think he's entitled to for that song? I'm sorry, but no."

Mavers sits back, adamant.

"No way."

I try to ask another question, but he's on an unstoppable roll now:

"I've thought about it, imagined the big 'court case': he'd stand up and say he wrote the music or melody or chords or whatever, and then it would be my turn to speak. I'd get up and say: 'So, Mike, you say you wrote the music and guitar chords for "Callin' All"?'

"'Yes,' he'd say.

"'Okay,' I'd say, 'So,' [*Mavers pulls an imaginary guitar from behind him, passing it to Badger, trapped in the witness box*] '*play* it for the members of the jury!'

"And that would be the end of it," says Mavers, with a look of triumph, "because he wouldn't be able to.

"I'm just trying to put the credit back to where it rightfully should be, la, that's all."

There is only one song in the small, officially released La's catalogue which has a writing credit other than a simple 'L.A. Mavers'. That song is 'Over', which is credited 'L.Mavers/J.Power' and now seems a good point to bring it up. But Mavers, still on his roll, is there before me:

"If you take 'Over': 'Of course', I said, when it came to credits on that, because John had those three or four opening chords and the initial melody. Originally it was: [*Mavers sings to the tune of 'Over'*] 'Old man, where are you going?' I took that and made it something else and added some other chords – but it was John's idea, so of course he deserved a credit. Of course, it's only right."

Gigging continued in earnest, with the band playing as often as possible and Mavers still unsure about their name.

"People would ask the name of the band, and I'd be like: [*quiet, side-of-mouth whisper*] 'It's "The La's"!'"

Mavers' muse began to flow in earnest.

"August the second – my birthday – 1986, I wrote the verses to 'Looking Glass' and a couple of weeks later wrote 'Liberty Ship'. I remember I was in town with my guitar and the main chords just came. Then, as I was trying to get the words, I remember this bus going by. On the side there was an advert for something and part of it was 'ALL MANKIND'. That was where that inspiration came from.

"As I remember it, we did some more recording but increasingly I was in control of the music in the band, and I know that he [Badger] knew that too. But Mike had [*pauses*]… I thought he was very spiritual at the time, and *we were* doing it *together* – it's just that my contribution was much more musical."

Despite the presence of the mega-enthusiastic Power, line-up difficulties continued.

"We still couldn't get a decent drummer. In fact, I had to do the drums on the 'Callin' All' demo myself.

"And Timmo [John Timson], who I knew from way back, was around then – he was seeing my sister at the time – and he started coming to a few gigs and he was like: 'I want some of that.' He was keen and we needed someone, so…

"The gigs started to come thick and fast, three or four a week, and we'd hang around in the afternoons and just jam and go back to Mike's."

But, according to Mavers, the seeds of the end of his relationship with Badger had been sown. He admits he threw a few:

"I can see now how increasingly I was dominating – because I was coming up with the songs – and Badger was beginning to feel sidelined.

But, you know, the songs were coming, that's just the way it was..."

He recalls the final gig with Badger which lead to their split.

"The Shaftsbury Theatre: I don't know how we'd got that gig, but we were there anyway. 'We'll do it!!' The night before, we'd done a gig in a place in Wales and a gig in Liverpool, both on the same night."

The La's apparently relished the challenge this presented (loading amps on and off vans and driving miles and miles there and back) but the night was soured by squabbles.

"The gig in Wales went really well, even though they didn't know us. I got the feeling that we were finally being taken seriously and the feel of the music was coming across – it didn't matter where you were from. After the gig, though, vans broke down and stuff. We had to get back to Liverpool in time and everyone was kicking off about the fact that we'd come out to Wales to play.

"Then, the next day at the Shaftsbury, we were unpacking and the rest of them are still moaning... and at some point I opened my mouth to him [Badger] and said something like 'The way you're going, you're not going to be around on Monday!' It was just an argument like any argument, do you know what I mean?

"It was all said with our backs to each other, and then Badger came up to me and said he wasn't going to stay around, and so I was like: [*assumed bravado*] 'Fine.' Then he was hanging around, waiting to go, and I got the feeling that he wanted to talk but, of course, like whenever you fall out with anyone, I *wanted* to talk about it but I wasn't going to go to *him*.

"It was just an argument. I went back probably three times to see him over that January – '87 – but, when it was clear he didn't want to come back, that was it and Hemmings came in."

Mavers had lost his one and only musical collaborator, against his wishes. A sign of the strength of his connection to Badger is revealed when, after pausing a moment, Mavers decides to let me into a secret.

"I actually went to see him [Badger] *after* Hemmings had joined as well... because... it wasn't the same after he'd gone. It just wasn't."

But Badger wasn't coming back to The La's. The new line-up featuring Paul Hemmings on guitar began rehearsing, mainly at his parents' house.[68]

"The house was massive and Hemmings had all the guitar gear, so he did sound good."

Mavers is uncharacteristically vague about Hemmings and his stint in the band. He's had the opportunity of reading my interview with him, and confesses:

"John was always keen on Hemmings, but I think I've *read* more in that interview than he ever told me, or we ever spoke about..."

The new line-up continued to gig. The band was rapidly gaining a following. "It was obvious that the places we were playing were just getting to be too small, and the offers of bigger gigs were coming in."

Mavers acknowledges the fact that, despite his mistrust of the music industry, he was looking, like any young, ambitious musician, for a record deal.

"Those bigger gigs we took, it was in line for trying to get a deal, I suppose. We were still rehearsing at Hemmings' and I'd got 'Timeless Melody' there. About February '87, that was. 'Feelin'' was next – I just recalled the riff that I'd played before, and... there you go. The momentum was still there."

Label interest began in earnest.

"We had loads of record companies coming to see us."

And Mavers was keen to be signed.

"I remember, I think it was Island or Chrysalis came to see us play at Hemmings' parents' place. I remember just virtually bypassing the band with my acoustic, just so we could get signed! Just sort of... [*Mavers mimes jumping up in front of someone and playing guitar very enthusiastically, right in their face*]."

He smiles and lets slip another confidence:

"In that, there's a lot of the story right there..."

In the end, Go! Discs signed them, and the band immediately moved down to London, all sharing a house together. From this time on, at least from Mavers' point of view, things began to go very, very wrong for The La's. One major problem was apparently the band itself – or parts of it. The Mavers/Power/Hemmings/Timmo line-up wasn't the 'four musketeers' which Mavers had always hoped for.

"I'd made sure that John was signed into the contract, because he'd been there and I knew what his motives were. Paul Hemmings had come in, mainly via John, but I wasn't totally happy there. And Timmo was just, well... he was interested in other things. We weren't that tight, the four of us. I did say that to Go! Discs when we signed. But they didn't listen... it was left that Paul and Timmo would be signed up properly later if they showed themselves to be, you know, committed."

The house Go! Discs had found for them in London left much to be desired.

"We were all on top of each other and the neighbours complained about the noise all the time – you couldn't pick up a guitar without the police coming round ten minutes later. There were other bands rehearsing as well, you couldn't get any peace. We all started to drift and I was just there on my own, in a way, with the music."

It's hard to get much detail from Mavers about events post-signing to Go! Discs, which is surprising, bearing in mind the amount of detail he has recalled already from the early days.

"It's just that, all the time we were signed, I recall it as just me and the music, and nothing really stands out..."

The label asked Mavers who he wanted to work with in the studio, but he confesses that his virtual ignorance of studios and producers meant he had no idea of who would work well, and who wouldn't.

"So they had a list and it was like: him, him or him? The first one was Gavin McKillop, who did the 'Way Out' sessions, and, well, it was just crap. It [the studio] was like a hospital – really clinical, no vibe at all, marble and glass everywhere."

Even the legacy of one of Mavers' musical favourites didn't lift spirits.

"The Who built that studio, I think. But it was fucking shite."

But didn't he tell Go! Discs what he wanted?

"All I ever did was tell them what I wanted, but it was never listened to. They'd start off: [*big record company city voice*] 'So, what do you want?' And I'd try to start to tell them, and I could see them switching off because it wasn't the thing they had in mind, it didn't fit with their 'plan'. But they were like: 'Yeah yeah yeah.' Sort of agreeing, but then they'd do what they wanted anyway."

It's hard to know how much Mavers' view and recollections are coloured by the course of events, but there's no denying the man's sincerity when you're face to face.

"Probably up until about 1990, I felt that they [Go! Discs] wanted the same thing that I did, but that we both didn't know how to get it. I know now that I was lying to myself, though..."

Cracks in the foursome of Mavers, Power, Hemmings and Timson were revealed only weeks after signing the deal they'd all hoped for. Whether Go! Discs was the villian of the piece or not, there was certainly a lot of misunderstanding between band and label at the outset, as a Mavers anecdote reveals:

"Probably about two months after we'd signed up, there was a meeting and I remember walking into Go! Discs – which was only just around the corner from where this house was where we were all staying – I walked in and it was all: 'What's all this? Why hasn't this been done? Where's he been? Where's the other been? What's going on?!!' And, I'm sorry to say, it turned into a slanging match. I said to them, 'Fucking hell! I told you when we signed up that this was the situation... I told you about this, I'm not a fucking miracle worker, I can't do it all on my own!!'

"But they were just: 'Well, you got to fire them then! *You've* got to sort it out!'"

Timmo left or was dropped, mid-tour. (Mavers: "The company instigated that, and they certainly weren't sad to see him go.") Not knowing any drummers in London, the remaining three La's continued as a drummer-less three-piece for a while, even gigging that way as and when duty called.

At the same time, the writing was on the wall for Hemmings. He left by mutual agreement, or otherwise. Mavers wasn't happy:

"I just... I never saw him, hardly... I mean, I want to put my *life* into something, and I can't do that with people who just aren't arsed..."

All this inter-band turbulence was isolating the group (what there was of it) from an increasingly impatient Go! Discs. Still to do any substantial recording, there were no royalties due. As far as the label could tell, the band had imploded soon after signing. Mavers and Power had decamped back to Merseyside, so the label stopped their wages shortly thereafter.

Mavers: "It was mad. There we were: we couldn't claim dole money because we'd signed the record contract, but we had no money at all, completely skint. I kept trying to get the band together with different people and *still* they weren't switching the wages on. It wasn't until Chris Sharrock joined on drums that they were happy and switched the wages on again."

Mavers' opinion of Go! Discs had begun to sour by this time.

"I was always 'the little Scouser' who didn't know anything and I began to feel that that was the way they wanted it. I felt that my input was never acknowledged or properly listened to. Take the sleeve designs for the singles: only the artwork for 'Way Out' was anything we'd suggested. Even then it was pretty far from what we'd wanted. Every other single, they [Go! Discs] just did what they wanted, put whatever they wanted on the front."

Mavers suddenly jumps from the past right up to date and tells me that he's so pleased not to be 'beholden' to any record companies or publishers now. He starts talking about his enthusiasm for the Internet, and even talks about advertising recordings there and supplying his music direct to those who want to hear. It's exciting to hear him talk this way, but then you have to remind yourself that a lot of the new material has to be recorded first. More importantly, it has to be recorded to Mavers' satisfaction.

He continues to outline his plan to get his music out. He talks about bypassing music shops and their mark-up – and the managers and their mark-up, and the manufacturers and their mark-up – and selling direct to fans with records he's had printed himself. You can almost hear the music industry quake. But will it happen? Mavers seems adamant.

"I think that if people are *shown* it can be done, then they'll believe it and try it themselves. Once it starts there'll be no stopping it. That's the only way in which the business aspect of this makes any sense or has any appeal to me. Nothing's done on merit these days. It's all about how much you can afford to promote something, how far you can push it until people are just bulldozed into buying something. People don't need that. If something's of enough merit, it will sell itself, people will seek it out on their own. When they realise it's cost half the price they expected, well, people are going to ask questions, la. It'll be the start of the end and the start of the beginning..."

Chapter Thirteen
The Oral History of The La's
(As told by Lee Mavers)
Part Two: Songs at the bottom of the ocean

"The whole problem can be stated quite simply by asking, 'Is there a meaning to music?' My answer would be 'Yes'. And: 'Can you state in so many words what the meaning is?' My answer to that would be 'No'"
– Aaron Copeland

It's all going better than I could've hoped. The ideal interview: I do very little talking. Lunchtime comes but Mavers shows no signs of running out of things to say, so we split my sandwiches between us and he carries on, stopping to check the clock on the wall.

"I thought it was later than that, la, it must be all the talking."

Following the addition of Chris Sharrock on drums, the wheels began to turn again and the new line-up rehearsed and, shortly after, played one of their first gigs, at the Royal Court in Liverpool. Then it was time to record again.

"I'd got 'There She Goes' in '87 and that was going to be the single. But we could only record it when we got a stable line-up again, so it wasn't until mid-'88 with Boo and Sharrock that we got down to it properly.

"We were there about two months going through everything with Boo and Sharrock, but the company [Go! Discs] had just put us in there and it was all half-arsed. Chris Sharrock was still learning the songs."

Go! Discs were now determined to recover as much momentum as possible and the band were promptly sent out onto the road. The departing Byrne was swiftly replaced with Barry Sutton and touring around the UK continued. By Christmas, Mavers was beginning to feel the pressure.

"Honest to god, we needed that Christmas break. It was beginning to be like being on a bombing mission: gigs, rehearsals, bits of recording. It was all dead rushed and my brain needed a rest."

After the New Year, 1989 saw the Sharrock/Sutton line-up begin its recording in earnest. They went back to the Attic studio where Mavers had recorded the songs which became his favoured demos, but he was destined to be disappointed.[69]

"We got back there, and it was the same engineer, but they'd obviously managed to get some more money from the council, which was great – for them. But everything had changed – the desk was different, the tape machine was different and everywhere had been done up, and something had been lost. It wasn't the same place at all."

But Mavers goes on to say that, even if that hadn't been the case, they probably wouldn't have got the right sound anyway because of continuing inter-band problems.

"I don't think I ever got Chris Sharrock to play anything right in the whole time he was in the band. Of course, the record company saw him as 'the cavalry' so they didn't want to know that it might not be working out."

Mavers had always had a clear idea of how the album would evolve, what tracks would be included and in what order. He shows me a little notebook with some scribblings in, and there. Amongst other thoughts, words and song titles is the artist's original vision for his album. This is made up of eighteen tracks (a double album) which, in order, are as follows:

Son of Gun
Freedom Song
Clean Prophet
Come In, Come Out
Way Out
Doledrum
There She Goes
Feelin'
Timeless Melody
IOU
Over
I Can't Sleep
Knock Me Down
Liberty Ship
Callin' All
Failure

Looking Glass
Who Knows?

"But, honest to God, not one of them songs has been done justice to.

"And that would all have been the first catalogue, and the second would have been the new stuff, and so on. I'm not even interested in singles anymore anyway: it's the whole thing, the whole form, that matters."

After the Attic excursion, the band settled themselves into the Pink Studio in Liverpool for what was to become probably the biggest La's recording fiasco (no mean feat considering the competition) with almost everything being scrapped after nearly four months of work.[70] Relations with the record company were sinking fast. ("Things hadn't been resolved since that first argument. When Timmo left, we were the naughty boys after that.") Although in retrospect it seems only fair to commend Go! Discs for its commitment, for giving the band another opportunity to record after the Pink Sessions, and for going to the trouble to get a vintage Abbey Road desk, with all its hallowed history, Mavers sees it differently.

"It was like: [*adopts harsh company-man voice*] 'The boy wants a Jaguar, GET him a Jaguar! He wants an old desk, get him an old desk!'

"If he [Andy Macdonald] was truly serious, we'd have done it. It *would've* been done."

Mavers becomes reflective:

"He maybe saw that it was just me, really, and the others were just doing, well, whatever. When he signed us, I'm sure he felt that 'here's a band with heart and soul' but that was so far from the truth, which I eventually found out myself."

It seems as though Power and Sharrock going on holiday, and Mavers *not* going did have some bearing on the rejection of that set of recordings.[71]

"I bumped into a mate of John's and he said that John and Chris had just gone off on holiday paid for by the record company, and I just got really unhappy because I felt that I was the only one really trying with the music. So when I went in for the playback while they were away, I listened and it sounded crap, so I said 'No'. I felt like, you know, I had to take control. I had to assert myself."

So, against the grain, it seems, if those who heard the sessions are to be believed, Mavers threw away the best version of The La's' album out of spite.

With the departure of Sharrock after the rejection of the Devon tapes, the next (and longest-lasting) line-up of the group began to take shape.

"Neil and Cammy had the practice room when we weren't in it, which was fine because they were working on their own thing. We got to playing and it felt great – better than music had felt in a long time. Cammy and Neil were dead tight musically by then. So I ended up asking myself why I was looking for other players out there, wherever, when what I wanted was right under my nose.

"And the next thing, after gigs and what-not, Steve Lillywhite comes down and the others are playing brilliantly by then, the band is really tight, and they [Go! Discs] start suggesting studios and stuff, but I'm just going along with it because I felt that *any* studio would capture the sound we had then. The band was so good, I felt like it wouldn't *not* happen if we started recording again.

"But once we got there – Christmas and New Year 1989/1990 – it was just wreckage all over again. Three months of working till the middle of the night, but it just didn't happen. The last straw was that someone found a dossier on me that had been prepared! I couldn't believe it!!"

Go! Discs had apparently authored a 'Producer's Guide to Lee Mavers.'

"It had all these things in like 'Likely to say no to this and no to that, likes this...' and that was just the last straw, I was saying 'to fuck with this' – not the music, but all the goings-on.

"I might as well have been on the moon" is how he sums it up.

"So they rang us up after we walked out, saying: 'Are you coming in to mix this or what?' I was like: 'You can't polish a turd, man.' And they said they were going to put it out anyway, so I just let them get on with it."

"And then we had a meeting just as they were going to put it out, where they basically told us that we were over a barrel and we had to accept the album coming out. They'd just put out 'Timeless Melody' and it came on the radio in the office and Andy Macdonald said: 'See!!' to try to prove his point. And then the song finished – I remember it was Capitol Radio – and the DJ said, ' That was Timeless Melody by a group called The La's... sounds a bit more like a *tuneless* melody to me.'

"And I turned to Andy and *I said*: 'SEE!!!'"

All this tension was affecting Mavers' friendship with Power.

"I knew something wasn't right with us and I wasn't surprised when he eventually said he wanted to leave. We'd do gigs and he didn't even look over at me. There used to be the thing, you know, where you're doing a gig and you – the band – are so *into it* that you check each other from time to time, just to see if they're feeling the same way. But that was gone, long gone, by the time he eventually went..."

The tension may well have had something to do with the emergence of Power as fledgling songwriter, where so far there'd only been one songwriter (proper) in The La's. But how did Mavers feel about his sidekick's musical excursions?

"I… we [the band] didn't like them, I think that's true. I didn't mind that one: [sings] 'Yes, I'm doing fine, yes, I'm doing fine…" [i.e. 'Fly On', which would eventually become Cast's 'Alright'] but I preferred the way we did it with him, stronger, more powerful."

I mention that some sources commented that Power's songs seemed lyrically to be addressing his relationship with Mavers.

"Well, if someone said to *you*: [*quoting from 'Alright' again*] 'Do you think I'd miss you? Do you think I care? Did you think I'd lay down and die? You never even try.' And then: 'If you lose your mind, then you lose you mind…' How would *you* feel?"

Despite the bad blood, I suggest that there was a special rapport between him and Power, lasting longer than any other La (except Mavers himself).

Mavers looks me straight in the eye.

"Put it this way, la: when you're young, you don't know what a true rapport is."

He recalls the final split with Power.

"The A&R people came in while we were in some studio and it was all like a 'big announcement': 'John's talked to us and he feels that he wants to leave the group.'

"And I just turned round and said: 'Sound. OK.' And they were just*:* [*mimes open-jawed surprise*]. It was coming, I could tell."

Whatever the details, things are clearcut as far as Mavers is concerned:

"If he believed, why did he quit? If you believe in something, you don't suddenly *not believe,* do you? I don't think, in the end, he liked being what he felt was second fiddle. It wasn't a case of that, it never was, but I know that's how he saw it." It's clear that Mavers, while maybe not taking a great interest in Power's post-La's career, is not totally unaware of it.

"I thought that record [i.e.'Alright'] sounded awful. I think, maybe, he knows a bit more now what I was going through with my own music. I don't know…

"The last time I really saw all these people – Badger, John, Hemmings – was at Badger's wedding the other year. He and I had had our fall-out second time round, but I thought, well, I'll go and try to put it behind us. And I saw John and I was like: 'Alright, John?' And he was: [*sheepish tone*] "Oh yeah… alright?" He was already slinking away. Tommy Scott was the same. Other people might feel like a leper, but I didn't mind."

It's a sad little image, but it serves to remind that Mavers is still very much the outsider, even amongst his peers. Although they might not want to acknowledge it, they all owe him a musical debt one way or another.

It's hard to know how to take Mavers at times. Some of the things he says about all these experiences are outrageous and unprintable, others seem to contradict known events. He'll look at you with a sly, enigmatic smile and you wonder whether or not, without realising it, you've missed something.

And yet the real revelations, when they do come, are often asides, made briefly and then lost as the conversation moves on.

Perhaps sensing that I'm become more aware of this as time goes on Mavers looks me in the eye at one point and says: "'Course, that's Lee Mavers talking, isn't it?"

All the while he sits talking, he gently rocks backward and forward.

There is the occasional odd moment, as when a car horn sounds somewhere outside and Mavers looks up.

"That's a signal," he says, and promptly disappears from the room. By and large, though, it's a frank reminiscence.

Talk turns to the chaotic time after Power had left and the album release was becoming a distant memory.

"All of sudden everything seemed to be beating a path to my door. Oasis were around and had talked about The La's and magazines were doing 'Where Are They Now?' things and it started to give me a bit of a buzz again."

At the same time, fate was once again about to take a hand in the career of The La's in an episode which probably outdoes anything in *Spinal Tap*.

"I'd not long got this house and we were getting it all done up and there was loads going on and then one day this letter comes. I open it and it says we [i.e. the band] owe twenty grand over some T-shirt problem from when we were in America!

"And I was like: 'Shit! What do we do?!' So I sat down and rang up a few places to get some gigs – and it was then that I really realised how easy all that side is. It's just laziness of thinking that keeps musicians from dealing with it. And so it was just: the number of gigs needed to pay off the debt according to how much you could make from each gig."

The La's were back together and on the road again. Sort of.

"I think people thought we were really going at it and it was all serious, but we were just having a laugh. We needed the money. Jamming on things with an occasional 'Timeless Melody' or whatever thrown in. It was bum notes and the lot – Cammy on the bass! We were just finding our way through it, really – crash bang wallop. But that was fine for me.

"I think some people see that as all part of 'The La's' History' but I didn't see it that way at all. It was just a bit of messing about really."

Mavers tries to sum up his feelings:

"The story of The La's is 'all for one and one for all': that's the story. It's there if you look. But the bottom line is that the album would have been done if everyone had wanted it to be.

"There were lots of times when I was going off to studios on my own, down to London or wherever, and staying in little hotel rooms on my own – a lonely time – just to try to get things done when others weren't interested. It was doing stuff like that that did me – the band – in, in the end.

"But… it's been a good learning curve, knowing how *not* to do things.

"I'd kill myself getting to a stage, you know? Even now," he muses.

"But for all that people want it [i.e. more music, another La's album] it might as well be some sort of wild animal that David Attenborough comes out to see every now and again!"

We start to talk about the new songs, and Mavers is exuberant. He's shown me a long list of new titles. There's more, apparently.

"There's probably about another half an album's worth on the go. I got another one last week. Surely that's prolific enough?"

I don't answer. It's not for me to judge.

"Even if that's all there was, la: [*pointing to the ideal track sequence set out above*] pick the bones out of it!"

You can't. The point is made, and made well, without boastfulness. After all, how can you 'pick the bones' out of a song like 'Looking Glass'?

"But… it's the new century and… things have come to something when you can look your name up on a computer and there's file upon file of stuff! It's incredible!" he marvels.

I pull out my CD copy of the Go! Discs La's album.

"Music," Mavers sits back, "is symmetrical, all symmetrical, and *that* [*pointing*] isn't. It's as simple as that. You can hear the structure in it, you can hear each instrument straining, but in the end there's nothing there, it all sounds the same, you can't hear it.

"It's just someone else's versions of great songs – the company's version.

"But," he says with quiet resolve, "that will be put right."

It's only the briefest of moments, but we sit in the silence after that comment, and you can almost touch the optimism in the air.

"I look at the last ten years or so, and people's values, and I see a great hand at play. The universe – what is life? All the early creation stories begin with 'at first there was a sound' and that's dead right. Look into a grain of wood and it's all one line, a big twisting circle where everything changes, but, as things take a turn for the worst, so they will turn back in the end.

"It's like football – I look at that and I see life, in a form. There's fair play even though referees can be biased, but if you stick the ball in the net three or four times, then no one can deny what you've done because everyone can see. That's all I want to do, stick the ball in the net again and again. And then people will have to fall in line, there's no other way...

"I spent some time in Morocco," says Mavers, "and there's a story that Arthur Lee[72] was over visiting once. One night, he was with some Moroccan friends he'd made. He started reciting this two-thousand-year-old American Indian chant and the Moroccans knew it – joined in and finished it off for him! That's what I'm talking about."

I ask about the songs and songwriting in particular. Mavers' eyes light up.

"*Now* you're getting down to it, la. Something just happens and you can look back on it afterwards and reflect on it. But there's nothing like *being there*, you know?

"It's survival writing in a way. All I want is a greater sense, something spiritual. Maybe it can be describing a memory, a memory of something in the future."

He sits back.

"I don't know, I don't know. I just know what I get out of it. It's all about lifting a thing higher, all for one and one for all, balance and equality. When I'm there, it's like every word can be malleable, everything can rhyme and does.

"The motive gets you there. It sounds mad but, when I'm there, it's almost like you can see yourself with a mortar and pestle, and the only light is the fire before you, and you could be anywhere in the world, at any time.

"The best songs just go Bang! And they're there. It's like a galvanisation when that happens, and you want it to last and last, but it probably only takes a couple of seconds."

He reflects:

"I just feel that the songs cry out for an audience. Even if I locked them in a trunk and threw them to the bottom of the Pacific, you know?"

And what does the writer really get from his songs and songwriting?

"For me, just knowing that it's no blind thing – life. Being in touch with a greater source. It's hard to describe…"

He pauses to think.

"I can't duck the responsibility, even if I wanted to – it's got to be done. I just don't hear many other things with that muse. It's like that pitch we talked about: it's not some gimmick, it's something that can heal, can take away the tension. It's bigger than any band or one person.

"I don't even think of myself as a songwriter, I'm just a guy who's caught some stuff, because he knows where to look…

"And lately, I just feel that everything portends well. After all, this is like the last vestige of anything magical, isn't it? I can't find much magic in anything else these days, can you?

"I can only [sub]scribe to something that's true, and I find truth in the music."

Taking a moment, he smiles.

"It's scary stuff, isn't it?"

Somewhere, a door bangs and the sound of chattering young voices signifies that Mavers' children are home from school, which means our talk which has now lasted hours, comes to an abrupt halt. A shame because I really felt that our discussions had moved up to what seemed to be the final gear.

Now we're getting down to it, la.

It only takes a moment or two to pack up my tapes and recorder and say goodbye and thanks to Mavers. Before I know it, I'm driving home.

If I'd known then that it was the last time I would meet him, I would probably have said something more, asked something more or maybe shaken hands goodbye a bit more firmly.

Epilogue

"It's tough having heroes. It's the hardest thing in the world. It's harder than being a hero" – Lester Bangs

"I just want to put The La's and music into a little box and leave it there. If something happens in the future, then it happens…"

"So you don't feel up to having another get together and talk about the music?"

"No, like I said. It's just the music industry and the whole thing around that. I just don't want anything to do with it all. I'm happy now, and that's the important thing for me – to be happy. I don't want to talk about music or The La's – I don't even want to *see* a book about The La's in the shops, let alone read one."

"You don't want to see a book about the band?"

"No, that's right. I've always said that. Don't you remember me saying that?"

"No, not really…"

"Well, you've probably forgotten. And, if you've forgotten that, then you've probably forgotten a lot of other things. Important things."

"But Lee, you know… we got together and talked about a lot of stuff. You saw the draft chapters and things I sent through for you to see and all questions I asked…"

"I was just helping you get it right in your own mind, for your journal or whatever…"

Pause

"Well, if that's the way you feel, then that's the way you feel. I mean, I'm sorry of course, but in the end it's up to you and… I don't want you doing something you're not happy with. Well, look, just… well, I wish you lots of luck and I really hope that the music happens again for you, if you want it

149

to."

"Well, if The La's are doing anything again, I'm sure you'll hear about it…"
Pause.

"OK, well, I wish you lots of luck for the future and I hope it works out for you."

"Yeah, you too…"

Post Script

"He loved New York. He idolised it all out of proportion"
Woody Allen, *Manhattan.*

In the driveway of Lee Mavers' house sits a decaying camper van. He mentioned it briefly during our discussions. Although he can't drive, he said, it was bought "a while ago" with a view to "getting out on the road with the band and doing it."

Today, with four flat tyres, a mounting rust problem, and an owner who can't drive anyway, Lee Mavers' camper van is in severe danger of assuming metaphorical status.

Running through the story of The La's like a deep vein is the thread of the unfulfilled promise, always threatening to surface, always waiting in the wings of even the worst show, the least successful recording session.

One of the last approaches I made to a potential source for this book goes some way to contrasting the differing views people have of The La's:

"You know, I don't see The La's as all that great. I definitely don't rate Lee Mavers as a songwriter at all. You know, he hi-jacked Mike Badger's band, took a lot of bits of Badger's songs – *which were great* – and then tinkered with them for ages and added a bit of his own stuff and, all of a sudden, he's the golden boy. No. Mavers knows the truth and that's why he's been so quiet, he knows that a lot of the reasons he's revered are the contributions of others, which he hasn't ever acknowledged. And I don't think he has the ability to get out there on his own and really do it. All this '*Ooohh,* the sound's not right, the vibe's all *wrong,* no-one *understands* my music' is just a front to stop people seeing the truth. It gives him the excuse to sit on his arse, do nothing, and still seem great…"

Was there ever a band that inspired such a diversity of opinions? Without endorsing the above comments, they do come from someone who knew the people involved fairly well, certainly better than I do. As with so much in this tale, people seem unable to agree on even basic details, such as who was in the band when. Everyone saw the accident, but they all remember what happened differently.

Proliferating contradictions are another part of the problem, another curtain obscuring the truth. The tiniest details of the story often seem most telling. Take, for instance, the issue of lyrics. Mavers made much noise over the fact that, when *The La's* appeared, the accompanying lyric sheets were very wrong in places. He particularly regretted Go! Discs' mistake on the transcription of lyrics for 'Liberty Ship', citing their apparent mishearing of the line "I am the captain of the love you gave" as "I am the captain of the *love brigade*." Mavers was incensed by this mistake, intimating he would never use such a phrase. And yet, such is the nature of the 'the details' in the story of The La's that there is more to the anecdote than meets the eye: on one of the early demos for the song, Mavers can clearly be heard singing the phrase 'love brigade'. Yet he denies the phrase was ever written, assigns the blame elsewhere.

The frustration voiced by many of the contributors and sources for this book adds to the lingering sense of unfulfilled potential. You can lead the artist to his camper van, but you can't make him get in and drive.

But, as many sources observed, the metaphor itself is deceptive. One in particular pointed out that, if Mavers actually threw his hat back into the ring again and 'got out there', perhaps there wouldn't be quite so much to talk about, to speculate upon.

We are left with a confusing collection of snapshots of Mavers: the blossoming songwriter, the inspirational bandleader, the focussed and adventurous musician, the truculent talent, the master of inactivity, the serial disappointer of fans and peers, the reclusive family man and the budding commercial revolutionary.

We could go on. Each man in his time plays many parts. But the part Mavers seems most unwilling to play is Fulfiller of Expectations, except on his own terms – and only he knows what those are.

I recall what the lads from the Crescent had said when I talked to them about their time with Mavers: "People said to us: 'You'll only be with him for so long and then it'll just end.' And it did." In a way, my experience is similar – and no less of a disappointment for its inevitability.

Perhaps there have been times during the book when I have been guilty of over-romanticizing the story of The La's. Maybe, on those occasions, where I saw 'artistic frustration', others saw laziness or lack of motivation or simple truculence. Maybe what I see as the magic of the band and Mavers' music, the pragmatists among you, fair readers, would reduce down to one bloke with a couple of good songs and a penchant for eccentric behaviour.

I think, in the end, The La's were the band that I secretly wished I could've been in. Because I couldn't, well, here's this book instead. I'm signing off with a renewed sense of musicality – I can't wait to get away from the word processor and back to my guitar, which has been sorely neglected. I feel like I've gone as far down this road as I can go. Now I've had a good look around, it's time to get back to the main road, my road.

The great thing, *the great thing*, about doing this book – and now leaving it when at last there's nothing more to say – is that the story is *not* over. It *may* be, but the final decision is Lee Mavers'. At least the subject of all my talk and analysis is still living, still writing, still singing, if only in his own home, for his own amusement. It would be a strange world indeed if artists were forced to interact with society and peddle their wares when they didn't want to. At least the *potential* exists for more music to come. I recall something that Barry Sutton had said as our talk was coming to an end:

"You should definitely call your book 'Volume One' because there's more to come. Definitely. The story isn't over yet..."

We La's fans live in hope.

The longer I observe the regular retrospectives in the music press and the occasional cover versions of their songs (at the time of writing, the latest is 'Timeless Melody' by Pearl Jam – of all people!), the more I become convinced that The La's have never really been away, not really. Perhaps, like some sort of musical golem, Mavers will revive them when the time is right.

The Top Five La's Legends

Every myth, the saying goes, contains a grain of truth. Often, this is hard to believe: some of the stories about The La's are downright incredible. But who am I to judge? Every now and again in the course of researching the book, I would come across a story about Mavers & Co which was so obviously daft and unbelievable, it had a certain measure of, well, comedy value. You have to grab your laughs when you can with a project like this.

I can take no credit for this little section, since I didn't make any of these fishy tales up. They were told to me. The idea of assembling them all in one place came from the publishers, not me: to have a frivolous apres-postscript which played to the fact that the 'mystery' of The La's – which, let's face it, means Mavers – is something which will probably never end.

Now I want everyone to pay attention here, particularly any libel lawyers who may be reading: nothing that follows is in any way an attempt at the truth. I will go further: I do not believe any of these stories have a basis in objective reality. I will go even further: I know that some of them actually aren't true because the people involved have told me so. In the spirit of fun, I leave it to readers to guess which is which. Some of the rumours have appeared in several forms, with slightly different twists and I've tried to include variations where possible.

I have not included those legends which have already appeared in the main text, as that would be repetitious. So you won't find the 'Sixties Dust' legend or any reference to the 'There She Goes as Heroin Anthem' debate here. Those, I think, were by and large exploded in the book proper although, in truth, they did have a kind of credibility. Perhaps 'credibility' is the wrong word, but... what I'm trying to say is that this section contains the 'no-hopers' in the chances-of-being-true stakes.

But what I do not want – and let me be clear – are mutterings and grumblings from 'concerned parties' to either myself or my publishers about any of the following 'tales'. If anyone feels obliged to take any of what follows seriously, they need to get out more.

With that out of the way, in absolutely no order of any kind, may I present as follows:

Legend Number One: "Mavers and the Monks"
This La's tale supposedly takes place during Mavers' 'wilderness' phase, i.e. mid-1990s. In need of rest and recuperation, Mavers departs the UK for foreign climes (some say Italy, some Greece). This may be at the expense of some kindly record company or impresario or not. Anyway, Mavers ends up at a monastery in the Wilds of Wherever, apparently on some kind of spiritual retreat.

So far, so plausible, right? Yes, well… the story then takes an odd turn: Mavers is subjected to all sorts of physical and psychological tests by the monks. After a prolonged examination, he is deemed 'OK' (whatever that means) and that his musical gifts are assessed as being 'on a par with Mozart'. He arrives back in the UK with a tape of songs put down during his sojourn. These are presented to some record company or other, who promptly put them in their safe.

Legend Number Two: "Mavers: the Paul Weller connection"
Several of the craziest stories stem, unsurprisingly, from the mid-1990s, when rumours of Mavers and The La's seem to reach an apex of silliness. The mud tends to stick better then: in a crazy time, what's one more crazy story? So it is that some of these persist when otherwise they might be shaken off.

This tale has Mavers, again, seeking retreat from… well, whatever – in Europe again: Venice, to be precise. He apparently spends some time aboard a floating home with (then) label-mate Paul Weller. Being musicians, they play and jam a lot. So far so good: a nice scene, isn't it? Getting-our-heads-together-on-the-river.

Anyway, Mavers comes home. Weller is on the cusp of (re-)launching his solo career. This begins with the success of his song 'Changingman' which goes a long way to rekindling the public's interest. Then Weller is caught up in the tidal wave of BritPop. However, all is not so well in Huyton: one source claimed that, when Mavers heard 'Changingman', he declared it 'his song', that Weller has 'borrowed' a large part an original tune of his.

In fairness (before the writs start flying), this was actually denied by Mavers during our discussions, but the background to the tale seemed to warrant its inclusion.

Legend Number Three: "Mavers in the US"
Mavers and the Hygiene Strike. This story relates to The La's brief tour of the US and Canada in 1991. Key to this tale is Mavers' unhappiness about his relationship with Go! Discs. The story goes that Mavers had no interest in doing the tour – actively didn't want to do it – and was determined to make sure everyone knew it.

He devised a scheme whereby he would not wash for the entirety of the US junket. The trip ran into several weeks and, legend goes, things became a little fetid on the tour bus. During one gig, Mavers' sock pops through a hole in his shoes, and starts to beat a wet mark onto the stage in time with the music, while young impressionable American fans at the front of the stage look on aghast.

Mavers on the radio. As is customary when promoting a new record, The La's undertook some promotional radio station interviews in the US. Mavers' subversive approach here, according to one source, was to "make the DJ take off the Go! Discs version of the album which he or she would be using, and make them say it was shit. Mavers would then produce a scruffy cassette from his pocket, and make the station put out the demos over the air."

Legend Number Four: "Power to the Patriots!"
You have to smile at this one. Taking place at time unknown, but seemingly before the final 'Neil & Cammy' line-up, this tale surrounds the cancellation of one or two La's gigs and the reason therefore. Now, the real reason that gigs were cancelled is apparently that Power had hurt his hand whilst trying to catch a falling beer glass in a pub, which unfortunately smashed in the process, thereby rendering him unable to play his bass for a time.

Straightforward enough, you might think. Enter 'the myth-makers' and the story takes a fantastical turn. In this version of events (put about, some say, by the band themselves), Power's injury occurs as a result of (wait for it) single-handedly fighting off a gang of neo-Nazis, bent upon causing fascist trouble and stirring up anti-English sentiment. A slightly different version finds Power battling a similar group of trouble-makers, who, this time, had been harassing a young girl. At least one person maintained that all this happened on a ferry, and the 'Neo-Nazi' version ends with Power being arrested 'for defending his country'!

Legend Number Five: "The Pete Townshend Connection"
Ask yourself: who could have produced The La's' album to Mavers' satisfaction? Brought it a successful conclusion? It's a tall order, obviously. One story has Mavers approaching the legendary Who guitarist to see if

he's up for the task. The focus of the tale here is not the fact that the approach was made, but how it was made. Rumour has it that Mavers took to playing football (with other band members?) in the street outside Townshend's house, taking time to summon the courage to approach one of his heroes. Eventually, Mavers knocks on the door. The door opens, but it isn't Townshend who answers.

"I was just wondering," says Mavers.

"Yes?" says the person answering the door.

"...I was just wondering... if Pete... was coming out to play?"

Acknowledgements

Where to begin? I imagine most people will skip over this small section, but this is where I get a chance to thank all the people who have given help or encouragement or both during the very long time it has taken to write this book.

A first vote of thanks must go to Mike Badger, without whom the journey might not have started – at least it wouldn't have started as well. Similar thanks go to Paul Hemmings.

A big thank you is due to Sean Body and Bleddyn "the" Butcher at Helter Skelter, without whom this book would be a lot more self-indulgent and less readable than it is today.

Much thanks to John Byrne who was not only one of my most friendly, helpful and interesting interviewees, but who also provided me with a big leap forward at a time when it was really needed.

Cammy and Neil provided easily the most laughs I had during any of the interviews, and that is something I'm very grateful for. I have always tried to focus on the positive, Neil, without shying away from the other… honesty *is* best. I hope you're happy with the result.

Both Jo and Nicola at Independiente and Rock And Roll (respectively) deserve a thank you for always being polite and helpful on the phone.

Barry Sutton also deserves a mention for the time he gave to his reminiscences, although subsequently he proved worthy of a place in the Anti-Acknowledgements (but that is another story). Mr X also deserves thanks… your secret identity has been preserved.

Best wishes go out to the lads from The Crescent, helpful and polite and with the stars in their eyes. Don't give up, you lot.

A big thank you goes out to Phil Hayes and Neil Robinson at the Picket, supporters par excellence of live Liverpool music and musicians. Thanks also to James Joyce (and Jeanette) for sharing his memories so frankly and making me feel right at home near the top of a tower block in the middle of Huyton.

Both Pete Frame and Penny Phillips were kind enough to respond to my letters, even though they couldn't help.

Someone who I must mention – but whose name, unfortunately, I do not know – is the young bloke I got talking to at The Munro pub after the Barry Sutton interview. Not only had he written his first book, but he'd then scrapped it to start straight onto his second! Talk about self-critique. The conversation was inspirational – it must have been for me to remember it so vividly. So good luck to you, sir. Maybe your next book has already been published?

Friends and true believers deserving of a brief mention are Andy (who would much rather I had written a book about the Stone Roses – sorry, dude), Nickster, James the College Yard Bluesman, Auby and Nel, Dazzy and Izzy and my old muso muckers, Mister 'B' and Jim. Also James 'the Bin' and Sylvain, these last two knowing more about all things La than, frankly, is healthy for them. Also, let me not forget to mention and thank Mark, who saved and resuscitated my computer when it seemed to have gone pop with the final draft of this book locked in its innards.

Thanks also to my various correspondents far and wide: Jason Lefler in the US, Pete in Perth, Paul Crane in the 'Pool, and Sean in the US who found a discarded *Mojo* in the New York Subway – I got your card! Also to John Welsh, who was one of the twenty people to turn up to see The La's at Stirling University.

Thanks also go to Anthony Cord.

I also want to mention here the people I was lucky enough to have as teachers: Vic Jackson, who taught me to have self-discipline in the work I do; Patsy Woodward, who taught me to always think for myself (the most important lesson of all); and the late, great Pat Dalton, whose memory still inspires me to strive to be compassionate and understanding.

To nip any appearance of sour grapes in the bud, I want to send a big thank you out to Mr Lee Mavers, without whose songs, NONE of this would have ever have started. You continue to be an inspiration.

Thanks also to the muse and the omens whose appearances were rare and fleeting, but always timely, too.

The only note of apology goes out to both Edgar Summertyme and Danny Dean, both of whom I made fleeting contact with and then promptly neglected until it was past polite to contact them. Sorry, fellas…

This book would not be in your hands now were it not for the support and love of my wife, son and eagle-eyed proof-reading Mum (thanks, Mum) and the love and inspiration given to me by my father when I was younger.

    A last 'thank you' goes out to all the people of Liverpool who were always friendly and kind and helpful (and forthcoming with an opinion) whenever and whatever circumstance I happened to be in. And also, thank *you*.

Anti-acknowledgements

I have come to realise during all this that no-one can undertake the task of writing a book about *anything* without a lot of help from a lot of people, and hopefully all those are present and accounted for in the Acknowledgements. On the other hand, I also came to realise that there are, likewise, those whose total lack of assistance made the job a whole lot harder than it needed to be, simply by being uncooperative. "The music business, by and large, are just a bunch of wankers – most don't even have the courtesy to return phone calls or reply if you send them a tape": so said one of my sources during the interviews for this book. While understanding his point of view, I don't completely agree with the statement but, as with so many things in life, there is more than a grain of truth in what he says.

A lot of my information for this book came as a result of hard work and playing amateur detective. I had no other way of approaching people than usually to ring them up or write to them out of the blue and say, "Hey, I'd like to talk about The La's if you can spare me an hour or so!" Some were sceptical, but most were prepared to give me the benefit of the doubt, and I hope their trust has been rewarded.

However, I did come to realise that there was almost a pattern of co-operation with the various people I approached. Nearly always, it was the people lowest on the 'Music Status Ladder' who were the most giving of their time and memories. Conversely, it was those further up that ladder who were the most unhelpful, people like those at *Record Collector Magazine* and the *NME* – supposedly a voice for modern music and its listeners. Also Andy Macdonald and others at Independiente Records, neither of whom could even be bothered to return my calls or reply to my letters. Also, Rob Swerdlow, manager of Cast, who is guilty of similar offences.

"Well," you might say, "They are very busy people. Who are *you* to them, ringing them up out of the blue?"

It's a fair point. I would reply simply by saying that the people who buy this book (and the person who wrote it) are exactly the people who, through buying records and being enthusiastic about music in general, have put these others in the privileged position in which they find themselves. I think *that* may have slipped a few minds in a few plush offices.

I'm not an Elvis fan *per se*, but I do recall an anecdote about him, which seems appropriate here. Some members of the Elvis stage crew were often trying to prevent the hysterical fans at his concerts from tearing his shirt of his back. He turned to them one day and said something along the lines of "Let them have the shirt if they want it: they put it on my back. If they want to tear it off again, that's fine."

And, with those wise words from the King, we shall leave it there.

Bibliography/Further Sources
The La's in print

To include a list of all the individual clippings and interviews and sources which were drawn on for this book would mean a Bibliography of such a size that it would be a contender for a chapter in its own right, so selectiveness here is essential.

Much as it galls me to say it after my comments in the Anti-Acknowledgements, the *Record Collector* feature on the band [issue number 226, June 1998] is one of the best introductory, in-depth retrospectives published, featuring lengthy interviews with Mike Badger, Barry Sutton, Paul Hemmings and even John Power. The article is also valuable because of its comprehensive discography, including noteworthy foreign releases. Also relevant (but fairly light – and now out of date) is their article and discography for Cast in issue 217 from September 1997.

I commend *Mojo* Magazine to all readers of this book and fans of music *anyway*, but they also did a reasonable review of The La's' career in their February 2000 issue (number 75) – which also featured an excellent essay on the life and music of Fred Neil, for those whose interest may have been piqued by my references to him.

For a more superficial look at the mythos of the band, then Q, issue 174 from March 2001, is a brave if slightly jumbled attempt to record the history of the group, drawing a lot on the *Mojo* and *Record Collector* pieces but also with a few new interviews. An earlier Q, issue number 51 (December 1990), features the interview with Andy Macdonald which I quoted from and also an interview with the band, right at the height of the 'album-hating' period.

Obtaining copies of old *NMEs/Sounds Magazine/Melody Maker* is an increasingly difficult task. Even though at least two or three large articles from these sources are pretty essential for the La's enthusiast, it seems far simpler to rely on the Internet than hunting around and paying high prices for original back issues.

The La's on the Net

There are several good sites dedicated to the band, principally 'La-zarus' run by Sylvain Murphy which can currently be found at: www.geocities.com/The_Las/ – this has viewable copies of many of the best band interviews from all sections of the music press as well as the retrospective material I have mentioned above and many downloadable songs, TV appearances and other trivia.

The La-zarus site has links to some of the other (slightly lesser) sites about the band which, hearteningly, are from all over the world, including Japan. The Viper Label site (see below) is also a minor but interesting source of information.

Of course, the Net is constantly changing and so what is correct today may be wrong tomorrow. As a rule, if in doubt use a search engine to check for you.

The La's on Record

At the time of writing, *The La's* is still available on CD in its original version [catalogue number 828 202-2] although perhaps soon to be superceded by the (ahem) 'remastered' version [catalogue number 5495662] which does include additional B-side tracks – unfortunately not all ('Man, I'm Only Human' anyone? 'Come In, Come Out'?) even though the entire album and original material B-sides could fit onto a single disc (who *makes* these decisions?)

Fortunately for those with time on their hands and money in their pockets, there is a Japanese CD version of the album [London Records POCD 1982] which contains all of the B-sides from the single releases *except*: 'Over' (a glaring omission), the alternate 'IOU' and the non-essential (in my view) early demos and remixes of 'Clean Prophet', 'Way Out' and 'Freedom Song.' However, as a plus it does include the original single version of 'There She Goes' and so listeners can judge the merits of the two competing versions for themselves on one disc.

In the *Record Collector* retrospective mentioned above, Barry Sutton made reference to a provisional release date of 2007 for the next Mavers/La's album. He mentioned this in our interview as well but Mavers himself did not. Whether or not there is any truth in the date, it's probably best to look on it as changeable (surely a given after reaching this point of the book!). If there ever is another new release, it seems very unlikely that it will appear on a major commercial record label, so the internet may be the best source of information. That's just my opinion.

All Cast's albums (four at the time of writing) remain available on CD and other formats. Their debut *All Change* contains the song 'Alright' which was first performed by Power with The La's under the title of 'Fly On.' The B-side to the group's second single ('Alright') contains Cast's version of Power's 'Follow Me Down' which was also performed by The La's. As this book goes to print Power's debut solo album *Happening for Love* is about to be released on the Eagle label.

The Crescent's debut album *The Crescent* is also now available on the Hut label.

Since starting this book, Mike Badger and Paul Hemmings' Viper label has issued two La's-related releases and, all questions of Mavers' happiness with those aside, they are:
Lost La's 1984 – 1986 Breakloose, Catalogue number Viper 2CD
Lost La's 1986 – 1987 Callin' All, Catalogue number Viper 8CD (which interestingly credits 'Callin' All' to "Badger/Mavers".)
The Viper Label website can be found at **www.the-viper-label.co.uk**. The site cannot, at the time of writing, take direct orders for any of their CDs, so those interested will have to purchase them from ordinary retailers.
The label has also released two albums by Badger in his own right: *Volume* and the later *Double Zero*.

The *Callin' All* release also includes the previously unheard Mavers original 'Tears In The Rain' which proves to be interesting, although not as evocative as its title might suggest.

It's hard to conceive of there being a third release in this series, but perhaps there is still worthwhile material out there (for starters, the early demo versions of 'Looking Glass', 'Way Out' and 'Come In, Come Out'). These two releases – the second volume in particular – are certainly a good place to start for those wanting to get a taste of the band's music and story other than through the official album.

The Viper release *Unearthed Liverpool Cult Classics Volume One* contains 'Don't Lock Me Out' credited to The La's and apparently hailing from the rehearsals at Paul Hemmings' parents' house.

There seems to be a steady flow of La's bootleg recordings for those who know where to look (I include myself in this shameful category). This in itself is encouraging but content and quality varies wildly. The truth is that The La's did so much sporadic recording here and there – especially during the earlier part of their career – that the result is an almost-limitless supply of slightly different 'demo' versions of Mavers' earlier songs. Fans must decide for themselves just how many demo versions of 'Son of a Gun' or 'Doledrum' they actually need.

The *Callin' All* Viper release does, to its credit, try to gather all the relevant material: most of the key demo versions and part of the now-legendary Picket show (fuller versions are available: just over half of the show is included on the Viper CD).

Many bootlegs are simple copies of live radio sessions or broadcasts of gigs, some of which are of interest, others less so. Tread carefully is the only sure advice (not that any of this section is intended to condone pirate recordings you understand, but I accept that a fan's hunger can be insatiable.) Of particular interest for fans (both in terms of content and sound quality) beyond the Viper releases are the Radio One Live Session and the Key 103 acoustic session, both of which I have referred to directly in the book.

The irony of all this though is that the really interesting stuff is nowhere to be seen – where are the copies of the abortive yet completed Devon/Mike Hedges sessions for the album? Where are the *interesting* studio outtakes? Alternate studio versions of the known songs, particularly 'There She Goes'? They may be out there but if they are, then people are keeping them very quiet indeed.

Further Listening

Grow Your Own La's Album!

Since the released version is so maligned, it seemed worthwhile to consider if a more acceptable product could be assembled from the available sources, official or otherwise.

I have used Mavers' own ideal track list as a template – but with the versions of each song I *personally* feel are the best available – to give an idea of what the official album missed. I have not discriminated against those inclusions which have perhaps slightly lesser sound quality, but the following are all totally listenable, and also everything included is 'out there'. Readers may have to search hard to locate some versions of songs, but that's all part of the fun, isn't it?

What follows is only my opinion. Readers are totally, completely free to disagree with my every choice.

Son of a Gun

First up and probably one of the hardest to deal with, due to the almost endless number of 'alternate' takes available. The accepted wisdom dictates that we must include the key original demo version which is included on the Viper *Callin' All* release. At least, that take has a freshness that many of the later attempts couldn't recapture – it also stays closest to the latin roots of the song. If readers want to be a bit more adventurous, the Key 103 acoustic live session version is a close second.

Freedom Song

'Freedom Song' is a bit of a curate's egg really, being virtually a solo Mavers performance anyway. The *Callin' All* original demo version (featuring Mike Badger) has a slower, more ominous feel than the official version, so diehards will no doubt favour it. In truth, it's not that different to the Go! Discs version.

Clean Prophet

Although it hails from the much-maligned Pink Museum Sessions, the released version is as good as any live bootleg. Available as a B-side to the 'Timeless Melody' single.

Come In, Come Out

Although there are some interesting alternate versions available on bootleg (including an acoustic version on the Picket Demo), I see no need to mess with the original, released as a B-side to 'There She Goes' with Mavers' and John Byrne's totally complementary guitars.

Way Out

I'm going to stick my neck out and select the 1988 'remixed' version which can be found as a B-side to the four-track EP edition of the first 'There She Goes' single release. The remix improves ever-so-slightly on the discrete charm of the original single version which is much more acoustic and organic than the final album take.

Doledrum

Bizarrely, I think the version the band recorded for a Dutch radio session in

1991 remains to be bettered – it trumps the Go! Discs/Lillywhite arse-up. This version achieves a comfortable, loose feel which the album version suggested but never really delivered.

There She Goes
Probably the easiest choice, since the original single version is almost impossible to top (unless you happen to be Lee Mavers). For those wanting more variety, try the US import CD single containing an extraordinary live version from the Chicago Metro – a slower, spacey-sounding Byrds-style interpretation.

Feelin'
For sheer power, the Radio One Session version (as referred to in the book) has to be included.

Timeless Melody
Another radical choice, but the acoustic version performed by Mavers and Power (with just an acoustic guitar each) on Canadian TV's *Much Music* (circa 1991) captures all the soulfulness of the song which endless studio takes couldn't get a hold on.

IOU
My choice here is available as a B-side to the 12" and CD single of 'Feelin'. Although the sessions produced by Mike Hedges were destined for the bin, this version of 'IOU' escaped and easily surpasses the album take. These sessions are, of course, alleged to be the best The La's ever did.

Over
If it ain't broke, don't fix it. The only recorded take of this song is the one La's recording everyone in the band can agree they all like. Available on the 12" and CD single for 'Timeless Melody'.

I Can't Sleep
A left-field choice, but I would opt for the Key 103 Radio acoustic session because everyone's playing is so fluid that the song actually benefits from the stripped-down approach, giving it a chance to breathe. Diehards will no doubt want to substitute this for the live recording from the Picket Gig, preserved on the Viper *Callin' All* release.

Knock Me Down
A dearth of alternatives (only a couple of duff live attempts) means that

we're stuck with the official version (the B-side to 'Way Out'), a poor option.

Liberty Ship
Get your rotten tomatoes out, diehards! The album version gets my vote here: short, funky and direct. True, it doesn't have Mavers' playing of the milk bottle, which the *Callin' All* version does (listen on your headphones if you doubt me!), but you can't have everything.

Callin' All
One of several early songs which exist in seemingly dozens of versions, I selected the Picket demo version (*not* the version included on the *Callin' All* release) because of the imaginative acapella harmonies at the start which demonstrate Mavers' readiness to experiment to get his songs across.

Failure
Although it's probably the worst of the entries in terms of sound quality, the Viper *Callin' All* live version from the Picket gives you Mavers' full-throttle grungy-rockabilly delivery – and it's quite something.

Looking Glass
Stick to the album version. While some might argue for the inclusion of the original (truncated) demo instead, no known live version has really been able to capture the full beauty of Mavers' emotional-fulcrum track. So hats off to Lillywhite for once.

Who Knows?
Interesting that Mavers chose this delicate but subdued song as the album's coda. Available as the B-side to 'There She Goes' – and nowhere else.

Finally, all of the following have been influential upon The La's and Mavers' songwriting so those delving further should endeavour to seek them out. Particularly relevant albums mentioned by Mavers and/or others have been indicated in brackets.

Captain Beefheart (*Clear Spot*, *The Spotlight Kid*, *Safe As Milk* and of course *Trout Mask Replica*)
Love (*Forever Changes* and the earlier *Da Capo*)
Bob Dylan (*The Freewheelin'* and *The Times They Are A Changin'*)
Bo Diddley
The Damned
Big Bill Broonzy

The Stranglers
Chuck Berry
The Who (*My Generation* and *Meaty Beaty Big And Bouncy*)
Robert Johnson
Muddy Waters
Bob Marley
The Beatles (*Revolver*)

Lastly and on a completely separate note, I cannot recommend highly enough the music of Nick Drake. All three of his albums (and the fourth, a posthumous release) are extraordinary in almost every way. The excellent *Way To Blue – An Introduction To Nick Drake* covers all four and could be the best seven or eight quid you're ever likely to spend.

If anyone has any comments on this book or any information or recollections they want to share about the band, then I can be contacted via the publishers and will endeavour to respond (eventually) to any post sent. Or I can be e-mailed at: **secretfeedback@viecos.fsnet.co.uk**

Take care.

Footnotes

1. Captain Beefheart – a hero to many. Books have already been written about him and more will, without a doubt. After single-handedly inventing (with the help of his Magic Band) psychedelic rockabilly blues in the mid- to- late 60s, he went on carving his own unique path through music until he announced, in 1982, that he'd "had enough" of that. Since then, he has apparently devoted all of his time to painting in almost total seclusion.
2. The Stranglers' bassist.
3. John Timson – or "Timmo" as he is referred to by everyone who knows him – pops in and out of the band line-up at this point, but is back full time at the point of them signing their record deal, later on…
4. When speaking to Badger about this track, he recalled that it was one of the first things Mavers had written on the guitar and also confided that, according to legend, Mavers came up with the chord progression whilst on the toilet!
5. Badger describes that night's performance: "Barry *was* Johnny Rotten that night, had had national health glasses on and a beret, and they were playing crazy music, really crazy music. And I remember Barry shouting at one point: "I'm gonna pass the hat round now!" And he threw his beret into the audience!"
6. 'Trees and Plants', 'Break Loose' 'My Girl Sits…' and 'Sweet 35' were Badger compositions, with the rest penned by Mavers, all of which (with the exception of 'Clean Prophet') would end up on The La's' debut album.
7. Home of the Cavern Club, need more be said?
8. According to Badger the original title for the album was to be the fantastic *Dole Pay Me For So La We Know*!
9. Badger also appeared (as musician) uncredited on the 'Demo' versions

of 'Freedom Song' and 'Doledrum' which appeared on the 12-inch release of The La's first single 'Way Out' in 1987.

10 This wasn't Badger's last brush with music. After quitting The La's at the end of '86, he formed a new band "The Onset" almost immediately. Badger describes their sound as "sort of punk Cajun" and the group went on to record an album *The Pool of Life*. Ironically, this was released in 1988, two full years before The La's' debut would see the light of day. It featured two songs which The La's had performed: 'Down at the Space Rocketry' and 'Trees and Plants'. At various times, The Onset's line-up included Paul Hemmings (see later) and Danny Dean, both of whom had been on the fateful council musicians' scheme. The Onset faded away eventually and Badger formed "The Kachinas" who had commercial success, gaining a support slot with Space just as that band were making it big. "True to form," says Badger, "After that, we did nothing else." After the implosion of The Kachinas, Badger focused on different media, and eventually had success with his "Lost and Found" tin-metal sculptures.

11 See the previous chapter. This was the gig with Barry Sutton and his flying beret.

12 See later on for more on this notable track, which was actually recorded at this time and then shelved until Go! Discs (or Mavers) wanted it later on. Hemmings recalls the recording thus: "It was the first time we'd ever played it. Lee had a couple of chords and so did John, and both of them had a few lyrics, and there it was. I just pressed play on this little tape recorder, and we captured a moment which we never got again."

13 Hemmings: "There was some mention, when someone had contributed maybe a chord or a line to a song, that they ought to be given some writing credit, but Lee was always adamantly against that. I remember one time when we were talking about this, he said, 'No, you should learn to become bitter, and then you can write *your own* songs…'"

14 Ridiculous as this might sound, it was one of the more persistent rumours which came to light whilst researching for the book. Whether it was invented by the music weeklies, or simply adopted by them because it fitted in with their image of Mavers as "the mad genius", isn't clear, but you can't deny the strength of the image of Mavers sprinkling this magic dust on instruments and recording desks in an effort to capture the sounds he wanted.

15 Influential 1970s/80s music programme which was responsible for showcasing many groups who would go on to greater glory.

16 Of fellow Liverpool band Echo and the Bunnymen. Defrietas is now sadly deceased.

17 See the previous chapter.
18 For those wondering what I'm on about here, modal tunings and scales feature heavily in Eastern and some styles of folk music, often where the piece of music centers around one note and the melody is neither conventionally major or minor in key. This style of playing has gradually spread into many Western forms of playing, particularly folk music (witness the work of people such as Davey Graham) and has from time to time wandered into pop music (e.g. The Doors' 'The End').
19 After Hemmings came back from seeing the world, he stepped right into The Australians, fronted by Tommy Scott. This was an embryonic version of Space, with whom Scott would have much success later on, but without Hemmings. He had left and, through Badger's friendship with Ian Broudie, eventually ended up in Broudie's band The Lightning Seeds.
20 Public Address system. PAs are the things which give bands most of their volume during a gig and through which vocals are usually sung.
21 Forming in the very late Seventies and lasting into the early Eighties, the Cherry Boys were well known at the time in their native Liverpool, but never really made a national impact. With Byrne fronting on guitar and vocals they recorded the delightful 'Kardomah Café' (notable Liverpool meeting place for the Sixties Merseybeat groups, including the Beatles, situated on the legendary Mathew Street) which made a tiny dent on the charts (Byrne: "I remember performing it live on BBC1 around that time").
22 At that time, Paul Hemmings and John Timson, respectively.
23 This seems to be the origin of the heroin rumour which has become attached to 'There She Goes'. Some sources maintained that not only the song, but in fact the whole *album* (when eventually released) was about drugs and filled with drug references. But this seems to be based on a choice selection and then interpretation of some lyrics – 'I Can't Sleep' ("I was laying on the line" and even the title of the track itself implying some sort of dependancy condition). 'Son of a Gun' ("Burned by the twentieth century... he's doing time in the back of his mind"). Anyone needing confirmation other than the say-so of people like Paul Hemmings, who were actually there at the time of the song's conception, simply needs to listen to the song itself. The joy expressed isn't chemically-induced, but comes from the soul.
24 More sophisticated guitar players are able to obtain this 'chiming' sounding notes by simultaneously striking and muffling the guitar's strings.
25 Middle Eight – that part of a song where the centre of the melody shifts

(traditionally for eight bars, hence the name) and resolves back to the chorus. A classic example would be the shift to minor key in The Beatles' 'From Me To You' ("I've got arms that long to hold you...")

26 See Mike Badger's recollections about this gig in Chapter 1.
27 This album was *Upwind of Disaster*. Sutton left afterwards but the band continued. Sutton: "They went on and did another record, which sounded a bit early-grunge, a bit proto-Nirvana."
28 See the last chapter.
29 'There She Goes' spent only four weeks on the charts and reached number 59 on this, its first release. Things would be very different on its re-release...
30 Never heard of the Library of Congress Recordings? In the early 1930s, the American government decided that it would be rather a good idea if the many forms of American 'folksong' – and indeed singers – were recorded. Minions of the US government's Library of Congress were dispatched to all corners of the country with enormous 'portable' tape recorders to capture anything and everything which might be of interest. There were many such minions, but two of the most famous were father and son, John and Alan Lomax, who had a remarkable series of encounters and discoveries, particularly in the Southern states. These included finding and recording one McKinley Morganfield, tractor driver at the time, later better known as Muddy Waters. Also, they managed to track down the legendary Leadbelly, who was then serving a term of imprisonment, and even had a hand in securing his eventual release which allowed him to take up his musical career once more. Much of their research also paved the way for the belated but unfortunately posthumous recognition of Robert Johnson. In short, remarkable times and remarkable men. Readers whose interest has been stimulated should seek out the excellent 'Muddy Waters Complete Plantation Recordings' recently put out on CD by Chess (MCA). Use the liner notes of that to guide you to further sources. It's really all worth a book in itself...
31 Several sources maintained that in fact Mavers had or had at least tried, to physically destroy the tapes of these sessions. Rumours persist that they managed to survive.
32 Templeton would eventually find his feet as the drummer in Liverpool's vastly underrated band Shack. Imagine this: you are one of the most talented songwriters of your generation and yet virtually unknown outside Liverpool. Such is the fate of Michael Head and his band Shack. After spending literally years battling everything from drug addiction to crooked managers, in mid-1999 Shack presented the world with one of

the best albums of the last decade and... nobody took a blind bit of notice. *HMS Fable* is rich with influences ranging from nursery rhymes and folk music through to the sky-high harmonies of the Beatles and Beach Boys and yet bristles with its own originality. Alas, the band slipped back into oblivion again following that but, as this book goes to print, have made a comeback with the release of *Here's Tom With The Weather*. Readers are urged, nay, *commanded*, to obtain their own copy of this and their wonderful, wonderful first album.

33 See Chapter 2, page 32 for Paul Hemming's recollections of this time.
34 The Chris Sharrock/Barry Sutton line up.
35 John Power to *Melody Maker* in 1990: "It was the first time we'd played it, the very very first time..."
36 Neil: "Doing all those interviews and saying all that about the album was the only way we had to tell our side. It felt like we had to clear our name, it was a chance to tell the truth."
37 One of the things Mavers was most insistent of during the round of 'promotional' interviews for the record, was that Lillywhite had used only 'guide' or 'demo' vocal takes of his voice, which contributed to the flat feeling of the record.
38 Comparisons were drawn in the music press to the similarity between the song and The Who's 'Can't Explain.' Chordal similarities come to the surface during the verse sections of the song.
39 It was this later version of the song which Go! Discs chose to re-release in 1990 rather than the original version but, when the song was re-released yet again in 2000, it was in the original mix.
40 Compare this version of the song with the Radio One live performance, see page 83.
41 At 6.03 mins into the song on the album.
42 At various points near the end of the song: "Sail away on the air waves...sail away on an ocean wave" ('Liberty Ship') and "Even the words they fail me...look what it's doing to me..." ('Timeless Melody').
43 Mavers' own vision of the *production* sound of the album must not be discounted either. He was clearly a willing studio experimenter given the chance, as John Byrne has attested. One can only speculate how far Mavers would have indulged himself in this regard if he'd been allowed.
44 Despite Mavers' half-fluffed, half-laughed first few words which can be heard at the start.
45 Barry Sutton had recalled: "Lee had this little acoustic guitar – a three-quarter scale-sized Guild – and he just sat down and did it, there it was, bang! This really beautiful song."
46 The last assault on the charts, 'Feelin'' would reach number thirteen.

47 This was the beginning of the chaotic mini-tour, see page 101 onwards.
48 Studio Two at Abbey Road was the studio preferred by the Beatles.
49 See Chapter Six with Barry Sutton's discussions for more detail – see page 66.
50 Eyewitnesses to the gig reported that Mavers and Power were 'squaring up' to each other and that it seemed likely that violence might result.
51 Power is referring to 'Fly On' ('Alright'), 'Follow Me Down' and, almost certainly, 'Fine Time' which was in an embryonic stage at this point, but performed by Power at several solo acoustic appearances after leaving the band and before Cast were properly together.
52 From Cast's 'Alright'.
53 From Cast's 'Back of My Mind'.
54 Mavers talking to *Sounds* magazine in 1990: "There's always been drugs since time began. You've got to get your rhythm out, and you either do it with drugs or without…"
55 See page 70.
56 See Chapter 4, page 47 – this seems to tie in with Mavers' indoctrination of The Crescent into unconventional tuning methods.
57 Very prestigious (and expensive) type of American-made acoustic guitar.
58 Joyce is not wrong here. 'Skin Up Yer Bastards!' became sort of the La's catchphrase, appearing on posters and merchandise during their career. There were even free badges and stickers bearing the slogan given away with limited edition copies of the band's final release, 'Feelin'.
59 Around these times: *So I Married An Axe Murderer*, *The Parent Trap* and *Fever Pitch* being just three examples of films using the song prominently. In fact, *Axe Murderer* featured *two* version of the song, The La's' original and a version by fellow Mersey band the Boo Radleys.
60 Barry Sutton also featured in the line-up for a couple of gigs around this time. When we met he recalled: "Those gigs were great. The band had just practiced a few covers really and they were off doing these gigs. Lee Garnet had met Lee and joined the band on guitar even though he hadn't been playing long. And then Cammy came along and he wanted to be in on it, but Lee said that he'd have to play bass – and he did! Imagine that, Cammy on bass! That's how keen he was to be in.

"Lee was much looser with the songs and the set and to me that was great. He also did some of the new songs and the audience was well into it.

"I remember one gig: we were supporting Dodgy. In the dressing room, we were warming up and playing acoustics and singing all these three-part harmonies .I remember the guys from Dodgy at the back of the room just: [*mimes open-mouthed disbelief*]. And then we went out onstage and you could hear people in the audience saying: 'Who's this then?' and then someone pipes up: 'Fucking hell! It's The La's!!'

"What a great night, we blew them away."

I asked if he meant the audience or Dodgy and he just sits back and laughs.

John Byrne (aka Boo) was also in the band for one of these gigs: "I'd gone round to see Lee, just because it had been a while since I'd seen him and I wanted to catch up. He opened the door and the next thing I knew I was ringing my wife from God knows where, telling her that I wouldn't be home until late! It was a good gig though – I was a bit afraid that I'd forgotten the songs and would mess it all up because there wasn't any time for any real rehearsal or anything, but in the end it was fine. Lee's songs just stay with you, I think."

61 At this time, probably Cammy and Neil, and maybe Lee Garnet.
62 These are the later sessions which Neil Mavers spoke of in Chapter 7, page 84.
63 The comparisons between Fred Neil and Mavers are not idle. Although several decades apart, their musical careers seem to share a common path. Neil wrote the wonderful 'Everybody's Talkin'' which brought him notoriety and, probably, a guaranteed royalty income for the rest of his life which, in turn, allowed him to do little else (although, unlike The La's, he did manage to make it past the one album mark. Just). Both seemed to share the same mistrust of the music business, deliberately slipping out of the spotlight and remaining elusive figures even to their contemporaries, but also very influential. It was with great sadness that I learnt of the death of Neil while writing this book.
64 This release is actually *Lost La's 1984-1986 Breakloose* on Badger's Viper label. See the 'Further Sources' at the end of the book.
65 Guitarists are often noted for their loyalty to one type of amplifier or another. Often they feel their amp is integral to their sound. The antithesis is the punk approach which Mavers is describing whereby, rather than plugging into an amplifier which is then recorded by a microphone, the guitarist plugs directly into the recording desk, giving no chance for the subtlety of the sound of the amplifier to play a factor in the quality of the guitar's sound. Yea, Punks!!
66 The Rolling Stones' 1968 album.
67 This is the gig mentioned at by Badger at page 24 and later by Sutton. Mavers: "I think he's [Badger] going a bit far with 'Barry as Johnny Rotten', but he *was* brilliant – the whole band were. I saw them lots of

times after that, but they were never a good as that night again."
68 These rehearsals would yield the recording of 'Over', see page 30.
69 See Barry Sutton's recollections of these sessions, see page 64.
70 See in Chapter 6 for Barry Sutton's version of events at this time, page 62.
71 See page 67.
72 Of Sixties psychedelic band, Love. Their album *Forever Changes* is acknowledged as one of the classic psychedelic Summer of Love statements. Liverpudlians are apparently fascinated by Arthur Lee. Badger and Hemming's Viper label has released a recording of Lee playing in Liverpool, backed by the members of Shack.

Other Titles available from Helter Skelter

Coming Soon

Smashing Pumpkins
by Amy Hanson
Initially contemporaries of Nirvana, Billy Corgan's Smashing Pumpkins outgrew and outlived the grunge scene and with hugely acclaimed commercial triumphs like *Siamese Dream* and *Mellon Collie* and *The Infinite Sadness*. Though drugs and other problems led to the band's final demise, Corgan's recent return with Zwan is a reminder of how awesome the Pumpkins were in their prime. Seattle-based Hanson has followed the band for years and this is the first in-depth biography of their rise and fall.
Paperback   ISBN 1900924684   256pp   UK £12.99

Love: Behind The Scenes
By Michael Stuart-Ware
LOVE were one of the legendary bands of the late 60s US West Coast scene. Their masterpiece *Forever Changes* still regularly appears in critics' polls of top albums, while a new-line up of the band has recently toured to mass acclaim. Michael Stuart-Ware was LOVE's drummer during their heyday and shares his inside perspective on the band's recording and performing career and tells how drugs and egos thwarted the potential of one of the great groups of the burgeoning psychedelic era.
ISBN 1-900924-59-5   256pp   £14.00

Suede
By Dave Thompson
The first biography of one of the most important British Rock Groups of the 90s who paved the way for Blur, Oasis *et al*. Mixing glam and post-punk influences, fronted by androgynous Bret Anderson, Suede thrust indie-rock into the charts with a string of classic singles in the process catalysing the Brit-pop revolution. Suede's first album was the then fastest selling debut of all time and they remain one of THE live draws on the UK rock circuit, retaining a fiercely loyal cult following.
ISBN 1-900924-60-9   256pp   £14.00

Everybody Dance
Chic and the Politics of Disco
By Daryl Easlea
Everybody Dance puts the rise and fall of Bernard Edwards and Nile Rodgers, the emblematic disco duo behind era-defining records 'Le Freak', 'Good Times' and 'Lost In Music', at the heart of a changing landscape, taking in socio-political and cultural events such as the Civil Rights struggle, the Black Panthers and the US oil crisis. There are drugs, bankruptcy, up-tight artists, fights, and Muppets but, most importantly an in-depth appraisal of a group whose legacy remains hugely underrated.
ISBN 1-900924-56-0   256pp   £14.00

Steve Marriott: All So Beautiful
by Paolo Hewitt and John Hellier £20.00
Marriott was the prime mover behind 60s chart-toppers The Small Faces. Longing to be treated as a serious musician he formed Humble Pie with Peter Frampton, where his blistering rock 'n' blues guitar playing soon saw him take centre stage in the US live favourites. After years in seclusion, Marriott's plans for a comeback in 1991 were tragically cut short when he died in a housefire. He continues to be a key influence for generations of musicians from Paul Weller to Oasis and Blur.

Psychedelic Furs: Beautiful Chaos
by Dave Thompson £12.99
Psychedelic Furs were the ultimate post-punk band - combining the chaos and vocal rasp of the Sex Pistols with a Bowie-esque glamour. The Furs hit the big time when John Hughes wrote a movie based on their early single "Pretty in Pink". Poised to join U2 and Simple Minds in the premier league, they withdrew behind their shades, remaining a cult act, but one with a hugely devoted following.

Bob Dylan: Like The Night (Revisited)
by CP Lee £9.99
Fully revised and updated B-format edition of the hugely acclaimed document of Dylan's pivotal 1966 show at the Manchester Free Trade Hall where fans called him Judas for turning his back on folk music in favour of rock 'n' roll.

Currently Available from Helter Skelter

Be Glad: An Incredible String Band Compendium
Edited by Adrian Whittaker
The ISB pioneered 'world music' on '60s albums like *The Hangman's Beautiful Daughter* - Paul McCartney's favourite album of 1967! - experimented with theatre, film and lifestyle and inspired Led Zeppelin. 'Be Glad' features interviews with all the ISB key players, as well as a wealth of background information, reminiscence, critical evaluations and arcane trivia, this is a book that will delight any reader with more than a passing interest in the ISB.
ISBN 1-900924-64-1   288pp   £14.99

Waiting for the Man: The Story of Drugs and Popular Music
Harry Shapiro
From Marijuana and Jazz, through acid-rock and speed-fuelled punk, to crack-driven rap and Ecstasy and the Dance Generation, this is the definitive history of drugs and pop. It also features in-depth portraits of music's most famous drug addicts: from Charlie Parker to Sid Vicious and from Jim Morrison to Kurt Cobain. Chosen by the BBC as one of the Top Twenty Music Books of All Time. "Wise and witty." *The Guardian*
ISBN 1-900924-58-7   320pp   £12.99

The Clash: Return of the Last Gang in Town
Marcus Gray
Exhaustively researched definitive biography of the last great rock band that traces their progress from pubs and punk clubs to US stadiums and the Top Ten. This edition is further updated to cover the band's induction into the Rock 'n' Roll Hall of Fame and the tragic death of iconic frontman Joe Strummer.

"A must-have for Clash fans [and] a valuable document for anyone interested in the punk era." *Billboard*

"It's important you read this book." *Record Collector*

ISBN 1-900924-62-5   448pp   £14.99

The Fall: A User's Guide
Dave Thompson
Amelodic, cacophonic and magnificent, The Fall remain the most enduring and prolific of the late-'70s punk and post-punk iconoclasts. *A User's Guide* chronicles the historical and musical background to more than 70 different LPs (plus reissues) and as many singles. The band's history is also documented year-by-year, filling in the gaps between the record releases.

ISBN 1-900924-57-9   256pp   £12.99

Pink Floyd: A Saucerful of Secrets
by Nicholas Schaffner   £14.99
Long overdue reissue of the authoritative and detailed account of one of the most important and popular bands in rock history. From the psychedelic explorations of the Syd Barrett-era to 70s superstardom with *Dark Side of the Moon*, and on to triumph of *The Wall*, before internecine strife tore the group apart. Schaffner's definitive history also covers the improbable return of Pink Floyd without Roger Waters, and the hugely successful *Momentary Lapse of Reason* album and tour.

The Big Wheel
by Bruce Thomas   £10.99
Thomas was bassist with Elvis Costello at the height of his success. Though names are never named, *The Big Wheel* paints a vivid and hilarious picture of life touring with Costello and co, sharing your life 24-7 with a moody egotistical singer, a crazed drummer and a host of hangers-on. Costello sacked Thomas on its initial publication.

"A top notch anecdotalist who can time a twist to make you laugh out loud." *Q*

Hit Men: Powerbrokers and Fast Money Inside The Music Business
By Fredric Dannen   £14.99
Hit Men exposes the seamy and sleazy dealings of America's glitziest record companies: payola, corruption, drugs, Mafia involvement, and excess.

"So heavily awash with cocaine, corruption and unethical behaviour that it makes the occasional examples of chart-rigging and playlist tampering in Britain during the same period seem charmingly inept." *The Guardian*.

I'm With The Band: Confessions of A Groupie
by Pamela Des Barres £14.99
Frank and engaging memoir of affairs with Keith Moon, Noel Redding and Jim Morrison, travels with Led Zeppelin as Jimmy Page's girlfriend, and friendships with Robert Plant, Gram Parsons, and Frank Zappa.

"Miss Pamela, the most beautiful and famous of the groupies. Her memoir of her life with rock stars is funny, bittersweet, and tender-hearted."
                                    Stephen Davis, author of *Hammer of the Gods*

Marillion: Separated Out
by Jon Collins £14.99
From the chart hit days of Fish and "Kayleigh" to the Steve Hogarth incarnation, Marillion have continued to make groundbreaking rock music. Collins tells the full story, drawing on interviews with band members, associates, and the experiences of some of the band's most dedicated fans.

Rainbow Rising
by Roy Davies £14.99
The full story of guitar legend Ritchie Blackmore's post-Purple progress with one of the great 70s rock bands. After quitting Deep Purple at the height of their success, Blackmore combined with Ronnie James Dio to make epic rock albums like *Rising* and *Long Live Rock 'n' Roll* before streamlining the sound and enjoying hit singles like "Since You've Been Gone" and "All Night Long." Rainbow were less celebrated than Deep Purple, but they feature much of Blackmore's finest writing and playing, and were one of the best live acts of the era. They are much missed.

Back to the Beach: A Brian Wilson and the Beach Boys Reader
REVISED EDITION
Ed Kingsley Abbott £14.00
Revised and expanded edition of the Beach Boys compendium *Mojo* magazine deemed an "essential purchase." This collection includes all of the best articles, interviews and reviews from the Beach Boys' four decades of music, including definitive pieces by Timothy White, Nick Kent and David Leaf. New material reflects on the tragic death of Carl Wilson and documents the rejuvenated Brian's return to the boards. "Rivetting!" **** *Q* "An essential purchase." *Mojo*

Harmony in My Head
The Original Buzzcock Steve Diggle's Rock 'n' Roll Odyssey
by Steve Diggle and Terry Rawlings £14.99
First-hand account of the punk wars from guitarist and one half of the songwriting duo that gave the world three chord punk-pop classics like "Ever Fallen In Love" and "Promises". Diggle dishes the dirt on punk contemporaries like The Sex Pistols, The Clash and The Jam, as well as sharing poignant memories of his friendship with Kurt Cobain, on whose last ever tour, The Buzzcocks were support act.

Serge Gainsbourg: A Fistful of Gitanes
by Sylvie Simmons £9.99
Rock press legend Simmons' hugely acclaimed biography of the French genius.

"I would recommend *A Fistful of Gitanes* [as summer reading] which is a highly entertaining biography of the French singer-songwriter and all-round scallywag"
– JG Ballard

"A wonderful introduction to one of the most overlooked songwriters of the 20th century" (Number 3, top music books of 2001) *The Times*

"The most intriguing music-biz biography of the year" *The Independent*

"Wonderful. Serge would have been so happy" – Jane Birkin

Blues: The British Connection
by Bob Brunning £14.99
Former Fleetwood Mac member Bob Brunning's classic account of the impact of Blues in Britain, from its beginnings as the underground music of 50s teenagers like Mick Jagger, Keith Richards and Eric Clapton, to the explosion in the 60s, right through to the vibrant scene of the present day.

"An invaluable reference book and an engaging personal memoir"
– Charles Shaar Murray

On The Road With Bob Dylan
by Larry Sloman £12.99
In 1975, as Bob Dylan emerged from 8 years of seclusion, he dreamed of putting together a travelling music show that would trek across the country like a psychedelic carnival. The dream became a reality, and *On The Road With Bob Dylan* is the ultimate behind-the-scenes look at what happened. When Dylan and the Rolling Thunder Revue took to the streets of America, Larry "Ratso" Sloman was with them every step of the way.

"The *War and Peace* of Rock and Roll." – Bob Dylan

Gram Parsons: God's Own Singer
by Jason Walker £12.99
Brand new biography of the man who pushed The Byrds into country-rock territory on *Sweethearts of The Rodeo*, and quit to form the Flying Burrito Brothers. Gram lived hard, drank hard, took every drug going and somehow invented country rock, paving the way for Crosby, Stills & Nash, The Eagles and Neil Young. Parsons' second solo LP, *Grievous Angel*, is a haunting masterpiece of country soul. By the time it was released, he had been dead for 4 months. He was 26 years old.

"Walker has done an admirable job in taking us as close to the heart and soul of Gram Parsons as any author could." **** *Uncut* book of the month

Ashley Hutchings: The Guvnor and the Rise of Folk Rock – Fairport Convention, Steeleye Span and the Albion Band
by Geoff Wall and Brian Hinton £14.99
As founder of Fairport Convention and Steeleye Span, Ashley Hutchings is the pivotal figure in the history of folk rock. This book draws on hundreds of hours of interviews with Hutchings and other folk-rock artists and paints a vivid picture of the

scene that also produced Sandy Denny, Richard Thompson, Nick Drake, John Martyn and Al Stewart.

The Beach Boys' *Pet Sounds*: The Greatest Album of the Twentieth Century
by Kingsley Abbott   £11.95

Pet Sounds is the 1966 album that saw The Beach Boys graduate from lightweight pop like "Surfin' USA", et al, into a vehicle for the mature compositional genius of Brian Wilson. The album was hugely influential, not least on The Beatles. This the full story of the album's background, its composition and recording, its contemporary reception and its enduring legacy.

King Crimson: In The Court of King Crimson
by Sid Smith   £14.99

King Crimson's 1969 masterpiece *In The Court Of The Crimson King*, was a huge U.S. chart hit. The band followed it with 40 further albums of consistently challenging, distinctive and innovative music. Drawing on hours of new interviews, and encouraged by Crimson supremo Robert Fripp, the author traces the band's turbulent history year by year, track by track.

A Journey Through America with the Rolling Stones
by Robert Greenfield   UK Price £9.99
Featuring a new foreword by Ian Rankin

This is the definitive account of their legendary '72 tour.

 "Filled with finely-rendered detail ... a fascinating tale of times we shall never see again" *Mojo*

Backlist

The Nice: Hang On To A Dream by Martyn Hanson
1900924439   256pp   £13.99

Al Stewart: Adventures of a Folk Troubadour by Neville Judd
1900924366   320pp   £25.00

Marc Bolan and T Rex: A Chronology by Cliff McLenahan
1900924420   256pp   £13.99

ISIS: A Bob Dylan Anthology Ed Derek Barker
1900924293   256pp   £14.99

Razor Edge: Bob Dylan and The Never-ending Tour by Andrew Muir
1900924137   256pp   £12.99

Calling Out Around the World: A Motown Reader
Edited by Kingsley Abbott
1900924145   256pp   £13.99

I've Been Everywhere: A Johnny Cash Chronicle by Peter Lewry
1900924226   256pp   £14.99

Sandy Denny: No More Sad Refrains by Clinton Heylin
1900924358   288pp   £13.99

Animal Tracks: The Story of The Animals by Sean Egan
1900924188   256pp   £12.99

Like a Bullet of Light: The Films of Bob Dylan by CP Lee
1900924064   224pp   £12.99

Rock's Wild Things: The Troggs Files by Alan Clayson and J Ryan
1900924196   224pp   £12.99

Dylan's Daemon Lover by Clinton Heylin
1900924153   192pp   £12.00

Get Back: The Beatles' Let It Be Disaster by Sulpy & Schweighardt
1900924129   320pp   £12.99

XTC: Song Stories by XTC and Neville Farmer
190092403X   352pp   £12.99

Born in the USA: Bruce Springsteen by Jim Cullen
1900924056   320pp   £9.99

Bob Dylan by Anthony Scaduto
1900924234   320pp   £10.99

Firefly Publishing: An Association between Helter Skelter and SAF

The Nirvana Recording Sessions
by Rob Jovanovic   £20.00
Drawing on years of research, and interviews with many who worked with the band, the author has documented details of every Nirvana recording, from early rehearsals, to the *In Utero* sessions. A fascinating account of the creative process of one of the great bands.

The Music of George Harrison: While My Guitar Gently Weeps
by Simon Leng   £20.00
Often in Lennon and McCartney's shadow, Harrison's music can stand on its own merits. Santana biographer Leng takes a studied, track by track, look at both Harrison's contribution to The Beatles, and the solo work that started with the release in 1970 of his epic masterpiece *All Things Must Pass*. "Here Comes The Sun", "Something" - which Sinatra covered and saw as the perfect love song - "All Things Must Pass" and "While My Guitar Gently Weeps" are just a few of Harrison's classic songs.

Originally planned as a celebration of Harrison's music, this is now sadly a commemoration.

The Pretty Things: Growing Old Disgracefully
by Alan Lakey   £20
First biography of one of rock's most influential and enduring combos. Trashed hotel rooms, infighting, rip-offs, sex, drugs and some of the most remarkable rock 'n' roll, including land mark albums like the first rock opera, *SF Sorrow*, and *Rolling Stone*'s album of the year, 1970's *Parachute*.

"They invented everything, and were credited with nothing."
                                            Arthur Brown, "God of Hellfire"

The Sensational Alex Harvey
by John Neil Murno   £20
Part rock band, part vaudeville, 100% commitment, the SAHB were one of the greatest live bands of the era. But behind his showman exterior, Harvey was increasingly beset by alcoholism and tragedy. He succumbed to a heart attack on the way home from a gig in 1982, but he is fondly remembered as a unique entertainer by friends, musicians and legions of fans.

U2: The Complete Encyclopedia
by Mark Chatterton   £14.99

Poison Heart: Surviving The Ramones
by Dee Dee Ramone and Veronica Kofman   £9.99

Minstrels In The Gallery: A History Of Jethro Tull
by David Rees   £12.99

DANCEMUSICSEXROMANCE: Prince - The First Decade
by Per Nilsen   £12.99

To Hell and Back with Catatonia
by Brian Wright   £12.99

Soul Sacrifice: The Santana Story
by Simon Leng   UK Price £12.99

Opening The Musical Box: A Genesis Chronicle
by Alan Hewitt   UK Price £12.99

Blowin' Free: Thirty Years Of Wishbone Ash
by Gary Carter and Mark Chatterton   UK Price £12.99

www.helterskelterbooks.com

All Helter Skelter, Firefly and SAF titles are available by mail order www.helterskelterbooks.com, along with all music books in print in the world. These titles are also kept in stock at the world famous Helter Skelter bookshop.

You can either phone or fax your order to Helter Skelter on the following numbers:

Telephone: +44 (0)20 7836 1151 or Fax: +44 (0)20 7240 9880
Office hours: Mon-Fri 10:00am - 7:00pm,
Sat: 10:00am - 6:00pm, Sun: closed.

Postage prices per book worldwide are as follows:

UK & Channel Islands	£1.50
Europe & Eire (air)	£2.95
USA, Canada (air)	£7.50
Australasia, Far East (air)	£9.00
Overseas (surface)	£2.50

You can also write enclosing a cheque, International Money Order, or registered cash. Please include postage. DO NOT send cash. DO NOT send foreign currency, or cheques drawn on an overseas bank. Send to:

Helter Skelter Bookshop,
4 Denmark Street, London, WC2H 8LL, United Kingdom.
If you are in London come and visit us, and browse the titles in person!!

Email: info@helterskelterbooks.com